MURDER AND MYSTERY
IN THE
BLACK COUNTRY

Harold Parsons was born in the Black Country in 1919 and is still active within the region, being Hon. Vice President of The Black Country Society, whose magazine *The Blackcountryman* he edited for over twenty years. He is a freelance writer who over the years has contributed to *The Times, Guardian* and many other newspapers and journals. His books about the Black Country include *A Portrait of the Black Country* and *A Thousand Events in the Nineteenth Century Black Country.*

D1178447

By the same author

Portrait of the Black Country
Warwickshire, History, People, Places
A Thousand Events in the 19th-Century Black Country
Substance and Shadow (Autobiography)

Murder and Mystery
in the
Black Country

Harold Parsons

ROBERT HALE · LONDON

© *Harold Parsons 1989*
First published in Great Britain 1989

Robert Hale Limited
Clerkenwell House
Clerkenwell Green
London EC1R 0HT

British Library Cataloguing in Publication Data

Parsons, Harold
    Murder and mystery in the black country
    1. West Midlands. (Metropolitan County)
    Black country. Crimes, history
    I. Title
    364.1'09424'9

    ISBN 0-7090-3699-X

Map artwork by Edenart

Photoset in Palatino by
Derek Doyle & Associates, Mold, Clwyd.
Printed in Great Britain by
St Edmundsbury Press Ltd, Bury St Edmunds, Suffolk.
Bound by WBC Bookbinders Limited.

Contents

To Joan

Acknowledgements

I have many people to thank in some measure for assisting me in gathering material for this book.

Former Detective Inspector Walter Fishwick of the Dudley Police, now in his eighties, gave freely of his time and hospitality; the Medical Officer at Newtown Hospital, Worcester, supplied information on Powick Asylum; Mr A.S. Hill, at the time of writing Head of the Dudley Teachers Centre, and Mr D. Brooks of Lye, Stourbridge, provided useful information, and David Philips, Lecturer in History at the University of Melbourne, Australia, gave permission for me to quote from his book *Crime and Authority in Victorian England* (Croom Helm).

The archivists and staffs of the Local History Departments of libraries at Dudley, Wolverhampton, Walsall, Stourbridge and Worcester gave invaluable assistance, sometimes over long periods, whilst Harpenden Public Library, Hertfordshire, kindly replied to postal enquiries.

Most important, the hordes of long-forgotten journalists of the nineteenth century, in particular, labouring in cramped courtrooms, deserve a special 'thank you' for their detailed reporting for *The Wolverhampton Express and Star, Wolverhampton Chronicle, Walsall Observer, Stourbridge Country Express, Brierley Hill Advertiser, Staffordshire Advertiser*, and *Berrow's Weekly News*, Worcester.

I am indebted to the Walsall Local History Centre for placing at my disposal a booklet, published in 1914, entitled 'G.H. Darby, Captain of the Wyrley Gang', an investigation by G.A. Atkinson with prefaces by Sir Arthur Conan Doyle and the Hon. G.A. Anson, Chief Constable of Staffordshire.

Finally, heartfelt thanks to my wife, Joan, who has accompanied me at every stage of research and manuscript preparation.

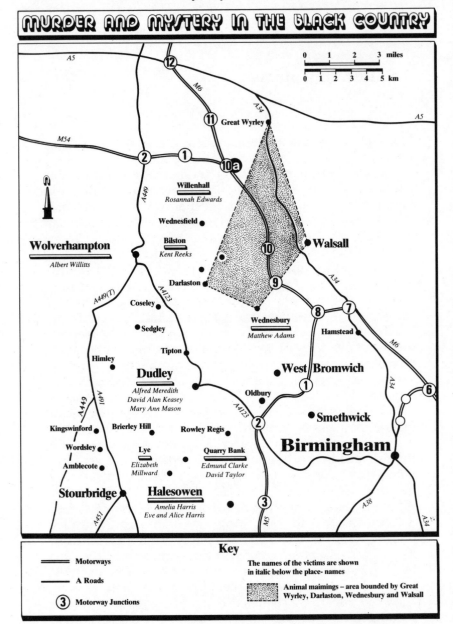

Introduction

Where precisely is the Black Country? For the benefit of readers who have no connection with the English Midlands some explanation is necessary, for the Black Country will not be found marked on any map. It lies roughly between Birmingham and Wolverhampton, but excludes the former, and takes its name from the once great south Staffordshire coalfield whereon the 'thick coal', as it was called, lay in deposits of up to thirty feet thick, along with extensive deposits of iron-ore, limestone and clay – all buried treasure awaiting the technology which would extract it commercially.

It was upon this mineral field in the eighteenth and nineteenth centuries, that there developed a plethora of ironworks and furnaces to make the region the workshop of the world, helped by the arrival of canals and railways to speed manufactured goods to world markets.

On the western side of the Black Country, in particular, these industries began to appear in the early stages of development alongside literally thousands of small nailshops and hand-made chain-makers – the so-called cottage industries which utilized the labour of men, women and children virtually day and night.

Across the dividing range of hills, on the eastern side, gun-makers, lock-makers, and horse-harness-makers predominated among the smaller trades, these too being originally carried out at home or within tiny adjacent workshops. One also finds in this book reference made to nailers, chain-makers, colliers and others, all sustained by a vast number of inns and beer-houses.

Overall, throughout the whole region, were of course the colliers, and it should be recorded as a matter of local pride that within the Black Country no women were employed underground.

The extremities of the Black Country have always been arguable and remain so today. However, for general purposes, we may place Wolverhampton at twelve o'clock and work around the perimeter in a clockwise direction through Willenhall and Walsall; down to West Bromwich at three o'clock, and through Smethwick and Halesowen; thence to Stourbridge at six o'clock, moving to Brierley Hill and Kingswinford at around nine o'clock; then back via Himley to Wolverhampton.

Despite a blurring of the edges, all the crimes dealt with here are beyond doubt in the true Black Country, with the exception of the so-called Wyrley Gang mystery, the focal point of which lay outside the region, but which had ramifications throughout, with animal maimings around Walsall, Willenhall, Darlaston and Wednesbury, and police officers from as far as Halesowen drafted in to help solve the mystery.

One other point of major interest should be made. Prior to the drastic boundary changes of the 1960s and seventies which led to the creation of the four Metropolitan Boroughs of Wolverhampton, Walsall, Dudley and Sandwell of today, the Black Country lay mostly in Staffordshire yet partly in Worcestershire, and that is why both Stafford and Worcester county gaols feature in these pages.

Considering the plight of working people during the nineteenth and early twentieth centuries, with poverty, overcrowding and drunkenness combining to fray tempers and create volatile situations, there were surprisingly few murders committed within the region compared to the present day.

Those detailed here are almost certainly the pick of the bunch for the period covered in terms of variety, location across the region, and interest created at the time. Only two of the crimes detailed were committed in what one would recognize as fairly affluent times.

Topographical change is such that none of the locations of these crimes is now identifiable, except for the street in

Wolverhampton where PC Willetts was shot (Chapter 11). Wolverhampton Street, Dudley, has altered little since the murder of a shopkeeper there (Chapter 5), but the shop itself has gone. As to the house at Willenhall in which a locksmith killed his wife (Chapter 6) there is no trace, yet I lived as a boy in Dudley at just such a house with an entry adjacent.

Quarry Bank still has its very steep High Street along which, in 1856, a gang of youths after a night out indulged in a prank which led to a death (Chapter 4); but on the Dudley side of Quarry Bank, at Merry Hill, there are enormous changes, notably the construction of a vast 'shopping city', larger than any of the surrounding towns, in part sited on what was virgin farmland.

Bearing in mind these changes, I trust that the crimes depicted here will succeed in evoking for readers the flavour of a relatively small, tightly packed region, still unique in a social structure whereby each locality retains an inbred isolation; although to a stranger the whole presents a continuous urban sprawl.

Harold Parsons
1988

1 Death on the Sofa, Quarry Bank, 1906

Ethel Clarke set out from her home at 18 Victoria Road,
Quarry Bank, at about 8.30 on the evening of Saturday 1
December 1906. She took with her two of her three young
children, leaving the eldest, aged five, with her
mother-in-law who lived across the road, and went
shopping. No! The late hour is not a mistake, for in the
days before refrigerators, when shops opened late as a
matter of course, traders were anxious to sell off
perishable goods cheap, especially on Saturday nights –
almost give them away, as the saying was – rather than be
left with them over the weekend.

Canny housewives like Mrs Clarke were in the habit of
waiting until near closing-time to 'snap-up' food bargains,
and without such a system many working-class families
would have fared even worse than they did; their plight
being grim enough as it was. For all that, Mrs Clarke was
nowhere near the bottom of the social heap.

Some three-quarters of an hour later, she returned
home with her children to find her husband, Edmund,
battered severely about the head and with his throat cut,
although his position was such that at first she did not
comprehend the extent of his injuries and was more
annoyed than concerned.

Three times – at the coroner's inquest, at the
magistrate's court and finally at the trial – she bravely told
her story. Her husband had returned home from work as
usual, tired after a hard day. After he had eaten the tea she
had prepared for him, he lay down on the sofa to have a
nap, telling her, 'Look sharp back. I want to go out.'

She had left him lying on the sofa, and when she returned was surprised to find that she was unable to get into the house.

The Clarkes' system of security is absurd to modern security-conscious thinking, though common enough at the time, and needs explanation. The front door had a latch on the inside, and in order to lift it from the outside a string was looped over it, passed through a hole drilled in the door and left dangling. Anyone could use it. There was a lock on the door but Mrs Clarke said that it was never used.

I am told that this practice was still prevalent in the 1930s, during a depression when most people had nothing worth stealing.

On this particular night, when Ethel Clarke went to pull the string in order to raise the latch, she found that it was broken. Whilst she stood puzzling over it, tut-tutting to her children in vexation, the door was suddenly opened from within by her father, sixty-year-old Joseph Jones, who lived with the Clarkes. He motioned her to enter, and as she did so she saw her husband on the sofa, in a sitting position, holding his head and bleeding.

'Father! What have you done?' she exclaimed.

'He started on me,' Jones replied, and she reprovingly told him that he ought not to have done it, still not realizing the truth. Without uttering another word, Jones left the house, determined in his intention, his fate already looming large in his mind.

Mrs Clarke went to her husband and spoke to him, but when he failed to answer, she brought forward the lamp from the table, and then, as the light fell full upon him, she saw the extent of his injuries and ran outside screaming, 'He has killed my husband!' and became hysterical.

Frank Hughes, a neighbour, was first on the scene.

Number 18 stood well back from the road behind a straggling hedge, the end house in a cul-de-sac (Pudding Bag Street in Black Country parlance). The front door opened directly into the living-room, which the Clarkes called a kitchen – in those days the sink would be in a separate scullery – whilst to the left was another front room.

It is necessary to describe the interior of this so-called kitchen. Indeed, so important was the position of everything in it thought to be that a land agent/auctioneer was subsequently delegated to measure the precise position of each item of furniture. Moreover, he was called as a witness at the magistrate's hearing and solemnly read out the measurements of the sofa in relation to the table, the fire grate and a bench commonly known as a settle – even the position of the clock and lamp.

Edmund Clarke, aged twenty-eight, by trade a master haulier and chain-maker, had been lying on the sofa, which was situated immediately behind the front door, beneath a window. One arm of the sofa was close to the fire-guard, the other arm being behind the front door, and it was at the door end that Clarke had lain his head. The table was only a few inches from the sofa, and on it stood a plate, knife and fork, and a lighted lamp. Opposite the sofa was the settle, a common enough item of furniture at the time. Blood was everywhere.

This was the scene that met Frank Hughes' gaze as he ran into the house. He instinctively caught hold of Clarke, who was barely alive, blood streaming from his throat, and thus inadvertently altered the position of the victim, so that he fell to the floor, his head near to the fireplace.

At this point PC Jones appeared, having been in the vicinity and heard something was amiss – bad news always travels fast. He was followed almost immediately by another officer, PC Maisey, accompanied, to the astonishment of the crowd that had been drawn to the premises, by none other than Joseph Jones.

It transpired that, after leaving the house, Jones had made his way to the High Street, a distance of barely 200 yards, where he knew he would find a policeman. Sure enough, there was Maisey, whom he knew. Jones went up to him and said, 'Take me to Brierley Hill,' meaning the police station there.

'What for?' Maisey asked.

'I've knocked his head in with a poker.'

'Whose?'

'Edmund's.'

Maisey said later that he thought Jones had had a drink but was not drunk. He accompanied Jones back to the house, not really expecting to find anything more serious than a family row that had resulted in blows. Shaken by what he found, he sent for a doctor and made a vain attempt to staunch the flow of blood, but medical evidence subsequently revealed that, even had a doctor been on the spot then, there would have been no chance of saving Edmund's life.

It was noted that, standing there in the tiny room, Jones made no show of concern at the spectacle of his dying son-in-law.

The doctor to arrive was named Fryer. He examined Clarke's injuries after Maisey had moved the table to give him more room, thereby nullifying those carefully taken measurements, and was quick to spot on the floor a square iron poker, bent and covered in blood, as well as two open razors, known, sadly aptly in this case, as 'cut-throats'. Clarke's throat was practically severed and his skull battered. It was clearly a most vicious attack. On the following morning the police found a third razor in its case on a shelf. This was also covered in blood, and the officer who found it must have wondered what kind of maniac killer would be so cold-blooded as to pack away one of his weapons so tidily.

By then, of course, Jones was safely locked up. He looked anything but maniacal and had slept for several hours that night, and again on the Sunday, peaceful perhaps that a deed for long on his mind had at last been accomplished.

Back to the night of the crime. Dr Fryer had Clarke's body placed on a cart for removal and noticed as the corpse was lifted from the sofa that the arm on which the head had lain had large cuts in the brown leather, resembling two sides of a triangle. Much blood had gushed into the stuffing and congealed.

Meanwhile, duly alerted to horrendous events in Victoria Road, Superintendent Johnson of Brierley Hill Police Station was hurrying on foot to Quarry Bank when he met PC Maisey with Jones in custody. He had a quick word but did not turn back, leaving Maisey and another officer formally to charge their prisoner with the wilful murder of Edmund Clarke. Jones made no statement.

Mrs Clarke and her children had been taken into a neighbour's house, she being at first too numbed to accept the fact that her husband was dead, despite the severe injuries she had seen in the yellow lamplight. The whole area was now buzzing with excitement, and some people recalled the last murder at Quarry Bank, committed fifty-one years earlier, at Wake time, when a man was fatally stabbed. (The Wake, a Black Country fair, was an important event in those days when 'King Alcohol' ruled, and henceforth that of 1855 became known locally as 'Stabman's Wake'.)

The annual Wake apart, Quarry Bank was a dour place, described at the time as a mining village – virtually the whole of the Black Country was at one time a mining area – although today Quarry Bank is best remembered for nail- and chain-making. At a nearby spot known rather grandly as Mushroom Green – 'Musham' to the locals – a nineteenth-century chainshop was restored and equipped with traditional equipment in 1976, so that on certain days visitors can still see chain hand-made.

Jones was brought before the magistrates on Monday 3 December, when Superintendent Johnson said that he had to apply for a remand until the 10th because on the following day the inquest was due to open. The prisoner, he said, would be brought from Winson Green, Birmingham, to attend.

The inquest was held before the South Staffordshire coroner, Mr T. Allan Stokes, at the Victoria Road Church Sunday School. Hostile demonstrations greeted the prisoner as he was brought in, and some women shouted, 'Set fire to him!'

Mrs Clarke now made the first of her court appearances, dressed in black. She told the court that she kept house for her father and that they had all lived together at No. 18. It had been her father's house until he had turned it over to her husband eight months before. Much was to be heard later of this transaction, but now the coroner switched to asking about events on the night of the murder.

'Was your husband lying on the sofa when you went out?'

'Yes, sir.'

'Was your father at home?'

'No. He hadn't been in since half-past-two in the afternoon.'

After clarifying that Clarke had been alone when she went shopping, the coroner turned to the business with the door latch on a string. When she found the string broken and could not get in, had she knocked? No. Yet her father had opened the door. How had he known she was there? He had heard her and the children outside.

'Suppose the string was not broken,' the coroner persisted. 'Anyone could have come in from outside.' She agreed this was so and that her father was aware of the fact.

The coroner then took her painfully stage by stage through the scene in the kitchen before returning to the matter of ownership of the house. 'Was he, the prisoner, obliged to turn it over to your husband?'

She said that he was, otherwise someone else would have had it.

'Was your father in money difficulty?'

She declared that he was, and to the coroner's suggestion that her husband held no ill-feeling against her father but that her father felt ill-will towards her husband, she agreed that was so. She did not know if her father had ever threatened her husband with violence.

'Did your husband tell you some time ago that the prisoner came upstairs with a chopper and threatened to chop his head off?'

'No,' she said firmly, and then went on to contradict her statement of a few minutes earlier. 'He had told me Dad had threatened his life.'

At that point the coroner asked Jones if he wished to ask questions, cautioning him that anything he might say could be used against him. Jones' questioning of his daughter was to prove a high point at each court hearing.

'Did I ever threaten your husband at all?' Jones challenged her.

'Not in my presence. But you have in other people's presence. My husband told me.'

'We have had words together about that affair of mine. That is all. I have never threatened him. But he had threatened me times out of count,' Jones told her.

Back now to the chopper, the coroner probing yet again to determine if Ethel Clarke had known that her father had taken a chopper upstairs and threatened her husband. She still insisted that she had not.

'Did you know about him threatening to throw a lighted lamp?'

'No, sir.'

The poker and three razors were now produced and Mrs Clarke confirmed that they were from her house.

'Was the poker bent as it is now?'

'No, sir, it was not.'

Samuel Clarke, brother of the deceased, who lived further up Victoria Road, testified to having heard Mrs Clarke screaming and had run towards the house, meeting Jones on his way to give himself up. No words were exchanged, the older man looking neither to right nor left.

Having told how he had gone for help, Samuel said that he had previously heard Jones threaten his brother, and he knew of the quarrel over the house. 'It was all over that, and money,' he declared.

Dr Fryer then testified that he had been called to the house at 9.20 p.m. and found Clarke lying on the floor, his throat cut in three places – two deep cuts, one superficial. One of the deep cuts had severed the jugular vein and windpipe. There was also two skull fractures. Clarke had died just as he arrived. He said he had made a post-mortem examination and gave it, purely ·as an opinion, that the victim's throat had been cut first, as he slept, the poker being used afterwards 'with tremendous force'.

After the various police officers had given their evidence, the coroner summed up for the jury.

'If you agree with what the doctor said, you will come to the conclusion that Clarke died from injuries inflicted on him. If you are convinced that they were inflicted by Jones, the only correct course to pursue is to commit, and that will be to commit him of wilful murder, because even though there may have been some sort of quarrel between them, the prisoner was not justified in what he did. It appears to me to be a cold-blooded and bad murder.'

The jury having dutifully returned a verdict of wilful murder, Jones was committed for trial at the Stafford Assizes, and as he was taken from the school, the crowds were three-deep, and on steep roofs and every vantage-point.

A relief committee was set up for 'poor' Mrs Clarke and her children, and collecting-boxes were passed round at the funeral. How poor she really was is a matter of conjecture, since her husband, a master haulier and chain-maker, had been somewhat above the average in that he had owned a horse and was proprietor of 'a wagon-ette or two' and a gig, and also a heavy cart which he had used to carry breeze – small washed coke for blacksmiths' hearths. He was also described as a 'saving man'. (It was by no means unusual for a man to combine two or more occupations, especially if one was seasonal, such as hiring a wagonette to take parties to local beauty-spots like Clent Hills or Kinver Edge.)

Tributes were paid to Edmund Clarke's high moral char-acter: he was a member of the church choir, he had taught at Sunday School and had been a member of a Bible class. After the funeral the vicar waxed lyrical concerning the victim's 'honoured and useful life' and of the wife robbed of 'a husband and supporter who would have been the com-fort of her days' and so forth.

For the resumed magistrates' hearing at Brierley Hill Police Station, Jones was brought from Winson Green. It is inter-esting to see how a prisoner on a capital charge was moved about at that time. In order to avoid further demonstrations when he arrived at Round Oak Station, the anticipated arrival-point by train, Jones was taken instead to Stour-bridge Station and thence by road to Brierley Hill.

The prisoner, a man of strong build with iron-grey hair and a moustache to match, grew more and more despon-dent as witnesses were called.

To the surprise of most people in court, Mrs Clarke proved more informative than before. She said that her father was a native of Pensnett (Dudley) and had gone to live at Quarry Bank some thirty years previously. For most of the time he had worked as a stock-taker or bar-weigher at the Netherton Ironworks. Years ago he had earned good wages and had bought the house out of his savings. Her mother had died in 1899, and since she was his only daughter, she had kept house for him and had continued to do so after she had married, when it was agreed that they should all live at 18 Victoria Road.

'After he finished work about two years ago, we kept him in food.' Was that what first brought discord in the household?

Under questioning, she said that her father had turned over the house to her husband in June 1905. Yes, there was a mortgage of about £100. Her father had turned it over because he was in money difficulties. She could not say how much her husband had paid her father for the house.

So Jones and his son-in-law had settled the matter themselves. Mrs Clarke said that she knew her father had received some money for the house, but it had not lasted long because he was addicted to drink.

She was asked: 'When your father wanted money, from whom did he get it?'

'My husband.'

'Would he often be asked for money?'

'Not very often, but he had done so in my presence.'

'Had he been given it?'

'Yes.'

'Had you ever heard your husband refuse?'

She replied that she had not, and this important line of enquiry was really the crux of the whole matter, for presently she was forced into admitting that after the transfer of the house there had been many quarrels over money.

Now the prisoner chipped in, loudly declaring that he was going to correct his daughter in what she had said. He said to her, 'As regards the money affair, of late the bother has not been over money. That was months ago.'

'Oh, but you've asked for money long since,' she told him. 'You know you have. We couldn't give it to you because of keeping the house and family.'

So she *did* know he had been refused money. Once again, as at the coroner's court, she had been rattled into a contradiction.

Her father went on to insist that the last time he had asked for money Clarke would not give him any.

The point well and truly made, Mrs Clarke was asked if there had ever been any talk of her husband's getting rid of her father. She answered, 'No,' and again Jones spoke up without any attempt by the magistrates to silence him.

'On Wednesday night the 12 November, didn't I come home, and wasn't your husband waiting up till I did come home, and when I came up the path and saw from the lamp in the kitchen that he was not upstairs, wasn't I afraid to come into the house?'

'No,' she answered. 'You were not afraid. He didn't do anything to you. He was afraid of you, not you of him.'

'I went and stayed in an outhouse,' Jones went on. 'Then after a while I supposed he had not come in, so I went in and took off my jacket and unlaced my shoes, but he started ...'

Here the magistrates stopped him and asked Mrs Clarke if she remembered the occasion, but she said she could not, whereupon her father renewed his attack.

'Did not your husband that very night start on me? Lay hold of me and pull me about all over the place? And didn't I say to him, "Loose me. If you don't, I shall take you to Brierley Hill police"?'

'You did something before that,' his daughter insisted. 'He hadn't done anything to you.'

Now Jones switched to a different tack. 'Didn't your husband set about *you* in my presence?'

Mrs Clarke's answer to this was an eye-opener. 'He didn't touch me to hurt me. Not anything to be brought to court for.'

'Why did you pull the poker out of the grate to him,' Jones persisted.

'I didn't hit him at all.'

'Well, what were you crying for?'

'There was a bit of bother between him and me.'

So Jones had uncovered an aspect of Clarke's behaviour to his wife as well as to himself. This inoffensive Sunday School, Bible class chorister and respected tradesman, was not all he seemed. How the courtroom buzzed! And how wise of the magistrate to let the prisoner have free rein in questioning witnesses.

The various other witnesses again trotted out their story, nothing new coming to light until Superintendent Johnson said that the prisoner had been to the police station before. He told Jones: 'I remember your coming to the station on one occasion and making a complaint that Clarke had assaulted you.'

How strange to find the prisoner's claim of ill-treatment, despite Mrs Clarke's reluctance to admit it, substantiated by a senior police officer!

Then came one Richard Llewelyn Province, who until the previous Monday week had held the licence of the Market Vault, Brierley Hill. He related how he had heard Jones threaten Clarke several times, although not actually in Clarke's presence. He had seen Jones on the Tuesday before the murder.

'He came into the Market Vault and said, "We have had another turn. Edmund came and punched me in the mouth while I was asleep. One of these times I shall go and knock his brains out." I did not take any notice because he had threatened so many times.'

The next witness, Joseph Pearson, an iron-moulder of Mount Pleasant, Quarry Bank, told the court that the prisoner, his brother-in-law, used to visit his house frequently. He recalled in particular a night some months earlier when Jones had talked about turning his house over to Clarke, saying that it was one of the worst things he had ever done. He threatened that one of these times he would chop Clarke's head off when he was asleep. 'I told him not to talk like that and leave the chap alone. I said, "If you've made a mistake, let it go by. You can't alter it."'

Asked if he had told Edmund Clarke of this conversation, Pearson said he had.

Jones was then asked if he had any questions. He

promptly challenged Pearson. 'Did I ever say any such thing as you have said now, as regards what I would do to him?', to which Pearson replied, 'Oh, yes! We've had everything over at our house. You, myself and my wife!' No love lost there, seemingly.

Now John Arthur Homer, a collier of Church Street, Quarry Bank, was called. He revealed that some months previously Jones had asked him if he would buy his house from him. 'I asked him what he wanted for it and he told me £250. I said I didn't want it. He then asked me to buy him a drink, and I did. As we parted he said, "I'll kill that b... Edmund Clarke".'

Enough had been heard to establish that Jones' hatred of his son-in-law had been festering for a long time. As to the witness Homer's refusal to pay the sum asked for the house, this was hardly surprising since Jones was undoubtedly asking too much.

The final witness to be called was William Hayes, a licensed victualler of the Church Tavern in Quarry Bank High Street. He knew Jones well and remembered his coming into the pub some three months earlier with a black eye. 'He told me Edmund had him on the sofa and held him there, and said that if he caught Edmund on the sofa he would give him one in return.'

These reports of constant moaning and uttering threats against his son-in-law were doing Jones no good at all, and the magistrates followed the coroner in committing him to the Stafford Assizes.

The wait was a long one, and in the meantime local worthies began to protest in print at the bad write-ups Quarry Bank was getting, in particular at a remark that it was a miniature Dante's *Inferno*.

'Quarry Bank,' wrote one irate councillor, 'was one of the most healthy spots in the Black Country, situated on the slope of a hill, with a perfect system of deep drainage, well lighted, with good wide streets ... a thriving, vigorous and healthy community. Reference had been made to tilted houses owing to mining subsidence (a common occurrence). That was largely a thing of the past.' In truth the good councillor was exaggerating, for no one can claim that Quarry Bank has ever been near the top of the list as a desirable area.

A year that is best remembered internationally for the devastating San Francisco earthquake and subsequent fire passed into history, and Joseph Jones languished in prison through the first two months of 1907 until his trial on 7 March before Mr Justice Walton (1845-1910); Mr F. Fitzgerald and Mr F.W. Sherwood prosecuted and Mr. R.J. Lawrence appeared for the defence. After the chief prosecutor had outlined the known facts, he concluded that there was evidence for the jury to come to the conclusion that Joseph Jones did deliberately design and intend to take the deceased's life.

Evidence given by the witnesses was much as before, although Mrs Clarke was driven to admit, under cross-examination by Lawrence, that her husband had slapped her on occasion and that her father had interfered to stop him. She further conceded that her husband had once struck her father in the mouth and that a policeman had called and warned about striking an old man.

PC Maisey, the officer to whom Jones had given himself up, told the court that there was previously nothing against Jones, who was a peaceable man but addicted to drink. On one occasion Jones had gone to him, his nose dripping blood and his lip swollen, saying that his son-in-law had set about him.

There was no sparing the effort at this trial, for the now famous sofa had been brought the twenty or so miles to Stafford and produced in court so that the tear in the arm, supposedly made by the poker, and the heavily bloodstained stuffing, could be examined by the jury. The kitchen table would probably have been brought also, but a policeman had put it outside to allow more space for the doctor, and rain had washed off most of the blood. As it was, a detailed plan of the room was produced, and even pieces of blood-spattered wallpaper, stripped from the kitchen wall, were on exhibit. The violence of the onslaught on Clarke was not to be left to the imagination.

A doctor took the stand to explain that the prisoner had been under his observation whilst in gaol, and he had seemed calm, with no sign of mental instability. Jones had told him that his life had been dreadful and unhappy owing to Edmund Clarke's conduct. On the night of the murder, Clarke had assaulted him and he had lost his temper.

Addressing the jury for the defendant, Lawrence said that, whilst it must be admitted that the prisoner had caused the death, the whole crux of the case showed that the crime was that of manslaughter and not murder. He contended that it was possible that the deceased had attacked the prisoner and that the tragedy had occurred through exasperation. Dealing with the alleged threats spoken of by the witnesses, counsel suggested that it was merely public house tattle and of no importance.

This was clearly the best possible interpretation, and it was partly effective, for after a deliberation of half an hour the jury returned a verdict of 'guilty' with a recommendation for mercy. Sentencing Jones to death, the judge told him that he would send the recommendation to the proper quarter but warning him not to entertain too great a hope that it would be successful.

The jury would not be unmindful of Jones' frustration, despite the presence of the gory sofa, for to have no money in those days was a catastrophe indeed and usually meant the workhouse, for old-age pensions were not introduced until 1908, when seventy-year-olds could benefit; the health and employment insurance scheme came still later, in 1911. As people have frequently commented, Joseph Jones was 'born too soon'.

How much Jones had received from Clarke for his

house was never disclosed, but with beer at about twopence a pint, one would have thought it would have taken even a heavy drinker more than eight months to get through whatever he received. Having to beg from his son-in-law, who treated him badly, would have preyed on his mind: he who had once been a home-owner and had money to spend.

It may be noted that his daughter, answering his questions in the various courtrooms, did not seem to rage at him for killing her husband, whom we now know ill-treated her also. Could it be that, once the shock of his death was over, she was not entirely displeased to be rid of Edmund Clarke?

When the Order of Foresters, of which Clarke had been a member since 1909, passed a vote of sympathy for Mrs Clarke and the children, it was again stated how very highly esteemed Clarke had been, but, alas, Brother Jones had been expelled from the branch in 1905, in that on three occasions he had committed a breach of the rules.

Despite the judge's warning to Jones about not placing too much hope on the jury's recommendation to mercy, surely clemency would be forthcoming, especially considering his age? But the death sentence stood and, moreover, efforts to obtain a commutation from the Home Secretary were unavailing. Perhaps that evidence of the sheer frenzy of the attack on Clarke was just too much to swallow.

However, a letter written by Jones to William Hayes, landlord of the Church Tavern, throws some light on his state of mind prior to the killing. Writing shortly before he faced the scaffold, Jones poured out his heart-felt feelings, and at this stage one feels he would hardly be likely to lie.

'During the last six years since my daughter's marriage,' he wrote, 'there has been more bitterness than during all the years before with my wife's parents, and my wife with me. There has been a bother day and night since my daughter has been married to Clarke. I only turned over the house to them so that Clarke would be kind to her ... I knew if I sold the house and left then she would have a nice [meaning horrible] life.'

Joseph Jones was executed at Stafford on Tuesday 26th March, a disillusioned and lonely old man, not visited once by any relatives during his months in prison; he who had spent most of his days getting up at 'three or four in the morning' to go to work, and who had lived to see his daughter married to a man who had forced him to sell his house and become an unwanted lodger, and begrudged him the price of a drink when he was out of money.

2 Revenge is Sweet, Dudley, 1855

Kates Hill, one mile south-east of Dudley town, stands at just over 800 feet above sea-level, the second highest point along the dorsal ridge that divides the Black Country, extending north through Sedgley almost to the boundaries of Wolverhampton. This hill overlooks the town's ancient castle, and there is still a Cromwell Street here, reminding one that during the Civil War Cromwell's forces besieged the castle from these heights, until the garrison surrendered. As part of the surrender terms, the castle had to be partially dismantled, which is why it is a ruin today, although partly lived in until a fire in 1750.

But it is another Kate's Hill street with which we are concerned, High Street (now Highview Street), in which stood, throughout the nineteenth-century and into the 1920s, a public house called 'The Sailors Return' – an unusual name for a hostelry in the English Midlands. (A directory survey of some 700 nineteenth-century Black Country pubs revealed the most popular names to be 'The Red Lion' (63) and 'The Royal Oak' (58).)

The Sailors Return is remembered for the callous shooting, on 12 May 1855, of Mary Ann Mason, aged seventeen, an attractive girl who worked as a servant at the pub, then run by a Mr Hunt and his family. Described as the daughter of decent, hard-working parents, Mary Ann had been keeping company for about ten months with one Joseph Meadows, a twenty-four-year-old whitesmith (or tin and silver craftsman) who lived in lodgings at Round Oak, Brierley Hill, some three miles distant. He was a native of Wolverton, Bucks, indicative of how at that time the Black Country was a magnet for people in search of work other than traditional rural pursuits.

Meadows had been in the habit of visiting Mary Ann at the pub and was there on the Friday night before the murder, when it was noted by the landlord – who seemingly had an eye on anyone who might lure away his prize servant – that she appeared to be trying to avoid his attention. Nothing was said between them and, having had a drink, Meadows departed.

At some time between six and seven o'clock the following morning, he came back to the Sailors Return, and the landlord, hearing his voice, went down to open the bar door. It seems that one could obtain a drink at any hour in those days, and it was not unusual for a licensee to be dragged out of bed in the early hours to serve customers, men working long hours and difficult shifts.

Meadows entered and ordered a pint of ale, which he carried into the kitchen, where Mary Ann – early to her tasks, as were all good servants – was busy mopping the floor. Shortly afterwards two miners who had just left work went in to have a drink. They had not long sat down before Meadows, regardless of their presence, produced a carbine (a light, short-barrelled rifle) from beneath his coat and coolly shot the girl. He offered no resistance as the police were hastily summoned.

Superintendent Jewkes arrived upon the scene. He was described as a stout, cheery man who looked more inclined to enjoy life than to catch criminals. His policemen are described in Mark H. Washington Fletcher's *Inns and Inn Signs of Dudley* (1952) as wearing tight-fitting blue coats with swallow tails, and top hats with sheet-iron crowns, supported by two strips of iron up each side of the hat, blue trousers in winter, white in summer.

When Jewkes took Meadows into custody, the latter told him: 'I have had my revenge, which they tell me is sweet, and I am satisfied.'

He also made remarks to indicate that his reason for

shooting Mary Ann was jealousy. He declared that he would never tell why he did it, and added later, 'I went last night with a carbine intending to shoot her, and also myself, but saw no opportunity to finish myself off. I was determined that, if I did not have her, no one else should.'

He revealed that Mary Ann's parents had cautioned her against keeping company with him, in consequence of an illegitimate child having been sworn upon him.

Joseph Meadows appeared before the magistrates on the following Monday – his face for some unknown reason, was partially covered with a handkerchief throughout the proceedings. A man of 'middle size' (five feet four inches), with small, dark, round-faced features, he made no reply as the charge was read out to him.

The first witnesses to be called were the two miners who had been in the pub at the time of the shooting. William Ingrams said that, after leaving work in company with William Robinson, he had gone into the Sailors Return and seen Meadows sitting in the kitchen with a jug of ale and some tobacco before him. The girl Mary Ann was cleaning the floor, but Meadows did not speak to her.

Ingrams said he was only a few feet from Meadows when he was startled by the report of a firearm. He saw the girl fall and observed Meadows with the carbine. Ingrams told the court that he had said: 'Oh, you rogue! What have you done? You have shot the young wench.' To this Meadows replied, presumably as a threat, 'I have another revolver in my pocket.' He was lying.

There being no legal advice for Meadows, he said when asked that he had no questions to put to the witness.

William Robinson then corroborated the evidence of his mate Ingrams, adding that, as he looked to see who had fired the shot, he saw the carbine on the floor. Meadows picked it up, and he took it from him and handed it to the landlord. According to him, Meadows said, 'She should have given me an answer.'

Robinson also disclosed that, during conversation prior to the shooting, Meadows had told him that he was having to pay 1s. 9d. a week towards the support of a bastard child.

Next to be called was William Hunt, the landlord, who told how he had let Meadows into the pub and served him with ale. Shortly after he had done so, Mrs Hunt had come downstairs, and he had gone into the malt room which adjoined the house. He had been to and from the malt room several times between eight and nine o'clock. (A malt room was a brew-house on the premises, there being few commercial brewing companies at that time.)

Hunt told how he had heard the shot and run into the pub. The girl lay on the floor, and Meadows stood by the fire. As he entered the passage, he heard his wife cry, 'Oh! Good Lord, he has shot her dead!' He then went and 'collared' him, and told him, 'Oh, you vagabond! You have shot your own sister.'

Sister? Yes, for Mary Ann and Joseph Meadows had practised the deceit of pretending to be brother and sister, and this was fully believed by the landlord and his family, for whom she had worked for about seven weeks. However, in the interim between the shooting and the court hearing, Hunt declared that he had heard to the contrary from the girl's father.

Hunt said that, as he took hold of Meadows, the latter told him that he had set out from his lodgings to do what he had wanted to do.

Questioned about the Friday night's events, Hunt said that the girl had tried to hide from Meadows. Whilst they were at supper, some person had called for ale, and Mary Ann had said to his wife: 'Mrs, give me the child and you go into the bar.' His wife had said to her, 'Don't you know your brother is in?' and the girl had replied, 'If he is, I don't want to see him.'

Superintendent Jewkes then related how he had charged Meadows with shooting Mary Ann, his 'sister', and how he had searched him and found a canister of 3¼ ounces of shot, a flask with about one charge of powder, and six percussion caps belonging to the carbine. The hammer of the carbine was down, and on the nipple was an exploded cap. It looked as if it had been discharged.

Whilst in custody Meadows had told him that Mary Ann was not his sister but a girl he had been seeing.

Richard Meredith, a surgeon, testified that he had found the girl being held in a chair by two women. She was bleeding from a gunshot wound in the left side of her face, under the ear. She had other wounds on her face, and he had extracted several pieces of shot. Although still alive, the girl did not speak.

Another surgeon, W. E. Johnson, then told how he had made a post-mortem examination at the Sailors Return that morning. It is interesting to note that it was normal in those days for post-mortems and inquests to be carried out in public-house premises. Indeed, it was the duty of inn-keepers to provide a room and clean straw on which to lay a body, and also a room wherein a coroner and jury could hold inquests. This was because of the high incidence of accidents in mines and ironworks – boiler explosions were commonplace – at this period when the Black Country was at the height of its industrial prosperity before the great Ten Yard coal seams began to give out or were hopelessly flooded. In 1855 Dudley had no hospital, nor had it until 1871. Nor did it boast a proper mortuary building until 1901, at last relieving pub landlords of their macabre responsibility.

The surgeon Johnson, having related his findings in graphic detail, produced some of the shot taken from the girl's body, and to the surprise of no one they were found to correspond with those found in Meadows' possession.

The evidence concluded, action moved to the Sailors Return for the inquest, at which the jury returned a verdict of wilful murder.

*

The trial opened before a crowded court at Worcester Assizes on 17 July, with Sir John Walter Huddleston (1815-90) presiding. (Well known on the Worcester and Staffordshire circuits, he had played a part in the famous Rugeley Poisoner case.) Mr Creswell prosecuted, and Mr Kettle defended. Meadows was dressed in a thick jacket buttoned over his chest. He pleaded 'not guilty' and, as before, kept a handkerchief to his face.

The first witness called was the miner Ingrams, who repeated his evidence. The only new fact to emerge was that the landlady, Mrs Hunt, had also been cleaning the kitchen of what he termed the beer-house. (The Beer-house Act of 1830 permitted any householder whose name was on the ratebook to sell ale without holding a licence from the justices, by payment of a guinea and the excise. The Sailors Return seemingly fell into this category, which is why the kitchen was used by customers and why Mary Ann was a servant rather than a barmaid. Only later would it have become a fully fledged public house.)

Cross-examined, Ingrams said that Mrs Hunt had just left when the shot was fired. However, the introduction of Mrs Hunt at this stage was to give the defence a slender peg on which to hang their case, for she had not been called as witness at the magistrate's hearing.

After a model of the Sailors Return had been shown in court, Mrs Mary Hunt was, in fact, the next witness to appear. She stated that on the evening before the murder Meadows had been 'in my house'. She had not seen him speak to Mary Ann, whom she believed to be his sister. At seven o'clock the next morning she saw him when she helped the girl to clean the kitchen. 'I was on my way to get a bucket of water when I turned and saw Meadows levelling the carbine. There was a flash close to my eyes.'

She then related how she had placed Mary Ann on a chair, where she died after about fifteen minutes. Her husband had grabbed Meadows, whom she heard say: 'Now I am satisfied.'

It will be noted that there is some discrepancy in the time of morning quoted by various witnesses, particularly the two miners. It may be, of course, that they were unable to tell the time. At all events, neither judge nor counsels queried the matter.

Cross-examined by Mr Kettle, Mrs Hunt said she had not given evidence before but had been asked to attend the trial. She revealed that Meadows had entered the pub on the Friday night with a man named Thomas Price, of whom, mysteriously, nothing more is heard. She had not noted anything peculiar in his conduct, but remembered saying to Mary Ann: 'He's the biggest sawby I've ever seen in my life.' ('Sawby' is an old dialect word meaning 'idiot'.) She had said this because Meadows had asked for another glass – implying either awkwardness or unnecessary fastidiousness; it was hardly a welcome request to a woman with a home to run between serving customers.

In making the remark, she declared herself mindful that Mary Ann had told her of her parents' unease about Meadows – her brother, as she thought. Nevertheless, she had to admit, 'I saw nothing mad about him.'

Enter now Joseph Rann, the Round Oak whitesmith to whom Meadows was articled, as he said, for four years, of which two remained unfinished. He was probably more peeved about this than anything, for in the mid nineteenth century articled apprentices were regarded as virtually the property of the master, and often treated as little more than slaves in return for the opportunity to learn a trade. Indeed, those who escaped from their master were frequently advertised for in the press, and a reward offered.

Rann said that on the Friday, although Meadows' right time to come in was nine o'clock, he had not arrived home until two o'clock in the morning of 12 May, in an intoxicated state. 'I went to bed and left him lying on the sofa. When I came downstairs at about seven the next morning, he had gone.'

Rann told how he had gone to see Meadows in gaol and had said to him, 'You've done for yourself now.' Meadows replied, 'I intended to do it before I left your house.'

The carbine, shot and powder flash all belonged to Joseph Rann, who was a member of the Dudley Troop of Yeomanry Cavalry: a most unfortunate circumstance for Meadows in that it placed a weapon readily to hand.

Under cross-examination Rann said that Meadows was 'much intoxicated' when he came home, and when he had seen him at midday next day in the gaol, he still did not appear to be 'properly sober'. A slender hope here for the defence.

The surgeon Johnson repeated his earlier evidence, under cross-examination revealing that one or two pellets had penetrated the girl's tongue, thus preventing her from speaking.

The evidence for the prosecution completed, Mr Kettle addressed the jury for Meadows. 'The gentlemen whom he addressed were doubtless called upon for the first time to perform a most painful duty. On their verdict depended the life of a fellow creature ... he would try to lead them into a path whereby they would be relieved from the anxiety of inflicting on a prisoner a terrible death.'

He continued: 'The case depends on two classes of testimony – words spoken and actions taken.' Kettle then seized on the fact that Mrs Hunt had not previously been examined in court, a circumstance which, he declared, went against the prisoner, '... as his advocate could not be instructed so properly as he ought to be'.

The evidence of Superintendent Jewkes also came under attack. It appeared that the officer had memorized his evidence and had not brought a copy of his deposition to court. 'This meant,' Kettle argued, 'that his evidence ought therefore to be cautiously received.' He speedily added that, of course, he did not for a moment mean to imply '... but what he gave it to the best of his ability.'

Now Kettle got into his stride in making the best of a

bad job. He argued that Meadows had been very drunk at two o'clock on the morning of the murder, had imbibed further at seven o'clock and was throughout in such a muddled state as not to know what he was doing. He went on to put forward a theory that Meadows had gone to the beer-house armed with a carbine merely to extract a promise of marriage and that, should the girl refuse, he would tell her he intended to shoot himself by way of frightening her into a favourable decision. The ultimate futility of a promise thus exacted would have been quite lost on him, besotted as he undoubtedly was.

Kettle further suggested that Meadows might have been holding the carbine carelessly and it had gone off, accidentally shooting Mary Ann. He then made what was perhaps the one valid argument, namely that there must have been a strong '... reciprocal attachment between the prisoner and the deceased, or why should she agree to pass herself off as his sister?'

Why indeed? The reason for this deception remained a mystery.

Having done his best – however flawed – to persuade the jury to acquit the prisoner, Kettle sat down without calling Meadows, and his lordship promptly set about demolishing the defence argument. Regarding Mrs Hunt's not having been called earlier, he said that, whilst it was certainly better to bring all evidence before the magistrates, it was not unusual to bring in late evidence, and in true judicial fashion he outlined an earlier trial to support the view.

As to Superintendent Jewkes' merely refreshing his memory from his deposition instead of bringing it to court, he thought the officer was in order. He then proceeded to go through the evidence and was so clearly against Meadows that he sternly told the jury that, although they might think of the prisoner's life, *he* ought to have thought of his victim's. He then gave Meadows a tongue-lashing before passing the death sentence.

The date of execution was set for 4 August at Worcester Gaol, and in the interim Meadows dictated several letters. One, to his brother, dated 26 July expressed a hope that: '... this awful affair will not take too much effect on you. I had rather you did not come to see me, for I am sure it would be a most painful meeting.'

More revealing was one penned a few days earlier to his master, Mr Rann:

> I entered the prison with a heart and conscience nearly dead to all feelings of remorse at my past life, and of the awful situation I am now in. I shudder to think I was so cruel as to carry out a deed against one I professed to love, and to send her soul into eternity without a moment's preparation.
>
> Oh, that the Lord had mercy upon her soul and mine, and forgive my sins ... I hope my untimely end will be a warning to all young men. I do confess I have acted very improperly at times, but I know you have forgiven me.

As he dictated the words 'Round Oak' in Rann's address, he could scarcely have failed to reflect on the excellent job-opportunities to which he could have aspired on completion of his apprenticeship, for this was a rapidly developing iron-producing area – as opposed to coal mining which had predominated for decades – and he would have been aware that in the very year of his crime work had begun on the construction of the Round Oak Ironworks of Lord Dudley. It began production in 1857 and was to expand and endure as one of the two foremost iron and steel works in the Black Country until closure in the early 1980s.

Meadows also had the nerve, if that is the word, to write to Mary Ann Mason's parents, addressing them as 'Dear Friends'.

> I know I have committed a most dreadful deed that man can be guilty of against God and you all, and especially against one that was a most kind and affectionate sister to all of you. I believe it has caused many aching hearts, but I hope and trust

it will be a caution to those that is given to lead a wicked and rebellious life like I did up to that time.

Had I not led that wicked life nothing would have happened. ... it is merely to show you all what drinking brings on ... One dreadful thing is added to another until at last under the influence of evil passions and the temptation of the wicked one (drink) I have done such a thing as would at one time made me tremble to think of it. By the time you receive this I shall have paid the fullest penalty of the law of man ... I hope you will take warning by my untimely end. Farewell, dear friends, till the morning of the resurrection.

He signed himself 'your unfortunate Joseph Meadows'. One can only imagine with what loathing this was received.

There was no letter to the mother of his illegitimate child and, although he was in the company of prison officers night and day and conversed with them on various matters, he never once mentioned Mary Ann beyond at one point saying mysteriously: 'They are not going to know everything.'

The execution was anticipated by vast numbers of people as a great treat to be watched and enjoyed. It sounds inhuman now but, although the authorities attempted to play down the actual date and time, throngs arrived outside the gaol each day to watch, often in drenching rain, for the erection of the scaffold.

During the whole of the Wednesday and Thursday workmen were busily engaged in laying the platform with planks, a process rendered necessary because of the unevenness of the roof. The erection of the 'drop' was deferred until the Friday night. Hundreds came from Dudley each day to watch these preparations and perhaps also enjoy the added opportunity to sample a train ride, for the Oxford, Worcester & Wolverhampton Railway (subsequently to be dubbed 'The Old Worse and Worse') passed through Dudley, having been completed barely two years earlier. Those who could afford to do so stayed overnight at local hostelries.

Interest in the event was even more widespread, and it was reported that on the Friday morning a private carriage had arrived with a party from Henley-in-Arden, Warwickshire, having travelled all night in expectation of the execution's taking place that day.

Berrows Weekly News, the Worcester newspaper, was moved to comment that it was '... painful to witness the excitement and unbecoming levity which prevailed'.

By eight o'clock on the Saturday, other prisoners of both sexes in Worcester Gaol had been lined up to watch the hanging, and no doubt to learn from it accordingly. The bell tolled, Meadows was brought out, retaining his composure, and executioner Calcraft went about his gruesome task.

As was usual, the body hung in public view for an hour, and during this time the 'thousands assembled below' continued to gaze on the swinging corpse.

The last hanging in Worcester's historic prison took place in 1919, and it was closed in 1922. The building was later used as a furniture store – even as a Spitfire factory during World War II – and, although not a listed building, it was recently hoped to retain it under a preservation order, but it was accidentally demolished through a misunderstanding in April 1987. Red brick houses now occupy the area of Kates Hill where the Sailors Return once stood, and it would take an extremely well-informed local to pinpoint the exact spot where Mary Ann Mason met her death at the hands of her lover.

One cannot but wonder why she and Meadows had pretended to be brother and sister. Was it necessary to deceive the landlord and his family lest news reach her parents, who lived a couple of miles away, that they were keeping company?

It seems from this distance of years that Mary Ann's parents, who incidentally made no appearance at the trial, had unwittingly sealed her fate in trying to turn her against him. Probably at first their objection concerned nothing more than the seven-year difference in their ages – more significant than now, for life-expectancy was much shorter.

Their hearing of the illegitimate child would have been the last straw as far as they were concerned. Yet Meadows had stupidly made no attempt to conceal the fact, even bemoaning his maintenance dues aloud to fellow drinkers within earshot of the girl he longed to wed and whom he would let no one else have.

Had she switched her affections elsewhere? Nothing of the kind was ever suggested. But if not, against whom was his revenge 'so sweet'?

3   £100 Rumour Leads to Murder, Wednesbury, 1841

In 1841 Matthew Adams was seventy-four years of age, give a year or two at a time before births were registered and certificates issued. Let us reflect on some of the events he would have heard of or witnessed during what was then almost double the average life span.

He was in his early twenties when the French Revolution cast its shadow over Britain. He saw the canal network constructed across the Black Country and the appearance of steam locomotion. He saw the 'great' Reform Act of 1832 come into being, and in that same year lived in dread during a cholera epidemic which claimed over 2,000 lives within a radius of only a few miles. He saw too – perhaps participated in – the numerous local riots quelled by Walsall troops sometimes supported by Dragoon Guards.

It is not known what trade he followed, but Adams was thrifty and in his old age owned a row of cottages at Delves Green, two miles from Wednesbury on the road to West Bromwich, in what was at that time a desirable area in comparison with the great sprawl of industry to the north and west. He lived in one cottage himself and let the other three: they were simple one-room-up and one-down affairs, his own having a pantry built on, which had a roof sloping to within eighteen-inches of the ground – a piece of home-improvement that was to prove his undoing.

Adams was, as we say, comfortable. Yet for all his striving and longevity he was hit fatally on the head with a hammer on his own doorstep during the early hours of 1 December 1841. On the same day Viscount Melbourne was writing to the Queen regarding a choice of names for the new royal baby, born on 9 November and destined to be Edward VII.

The crime was set in motion when one Thomas Boswell, a twenty-one-year-old awl-blade maker, heard on the grapevine that Matthew Adams' granddaughter was about to marry. Adams had promised her £100 as a 'marriage portion' – £100 was an immense fortune at a time when a collier earned about 2s. 4d. a day, when a 4lb loaf cost 5½d., ale 1s. 5d. a gallon, and coal 7s. 6d. a ton, the whole region being built on it, along with ironstone and limestone.

Boswell quickly passed the word to his cronies, crooked to a man – the brothers Joseph and James Wilkes, aged seventeen and twenty-five respectively, and George Giles, aged twenty-one. It was an opportunity too good to miss.

They made their way to Delves Green at about one o'clock on the morning of 1 December. Having cased the joint, so to speak, they hit on the idea of removing the tiles from the sloping pantry roof – which they could do quite easily without even having to climb – and quickly made a hole large enough to get through.

As three of them scrambled into the pantry, leaving Giles to keep watch in the lane, the old man upstairs must have heard a noise, because, unhappily for him, he came downstairs. Hearing him on the move, Boswell sent the others round to the front door, and as he went, Joseph Wilkes picked up a hammer he found in the pantry. He pushed on the front door, found Adams behind it and struck him several violent blows.

Why the trio did not go directly from the pantry into the house, history does not record, but it made little difference, for the prize was too great to let a frail old man stand in their way.

However, Adams' next-door neighbour, Sarah Rollason,

had also heard a noise and gone to her bedroom window, opening the casement. She saw three men come round from the back of Adams' house to the front. It was a clear moonlight night and she could see that one had on a smock-frock whilst the others wore dark suits. She could not identify them later but said that the one in the smock (Joseph Wilkes) had gone to the door and tried to push it open, whereupon Adams opened it. She saw the hammer raised and heard Adams cry out. She yelled to them to stop and was cursed and threatened. One threw a stone which missed. She shouted 'Murder!', quickly roused her husband and dashed outdoors.

Alexander Brown, a labourer living next door but one to Adams, heard Sarah's cry and sprang out of bed, running into the street in his nightshirt, followed by four lodgers. By this time Boswell and his cronies had decided it was time to make themselves scarce and fled, so Brown entered through the hole in the pantry roof and came upon Adams from behind as he stood helpless at his front door, still gripping the latch, for instead of lying in a crumpled heap, as one might expect, he had managed, despite his injuries, to refasten the door.

In the darkness Brown asked, 'Matthew, are you hurt?' He opened the door to admit Mrs Rollason and the men gathered outside.

It was noted that Adams had armed himself with a pike (a long pole with a metal point) but had not had a chance to use it. The men helped to get him into Sarah Rollason's house, and as he was taken out he said, 'Lock the door.'

Mindful of his possessions to the last, those were the only words he was to speak, and he died at seven o'clock that evening.

John Adams, Matthew's son, was sent for and hurried from the public house he kept at Tame Bridge, about half a mile away. He found his father standing by the fire in Rollason's house and said later that he did not know if his father knew him as he helped place him on the chair upon which he was to expire. No attempt was made to get him to bed, and when a doctor arrived he turned out to be only an assistant and could do nothing for him. Neither could the surgeon, Thomas Pitt, when he arrived later in the day.

Medical knowledge towards the middle years of the last century was primitive and there were no hospitals – Walsall did not have its first cottage hospital until twenty-years later, and then it was only a small house in Bridge Street, with eight beds. Considering that this was one of the earliest of its kind anywhere in the country, there was clearly little to be done for poor Adams.

John Adams spent some of the time waiting for his father to die by going into the pantry and searching beneath the hole made by the criminals. He found a percussion pistol loaded to within a half-inch of the muzzle, and he asked a man who had come to the house, George Brown, to withdraw the charge and so make it safe. Brown did so and returned it to John, who, before placing it in his pocket, took the precaution of making a mark on the pistol and the percussion cap for later identification.

Enter now one Samuel Heatherley, by trade a baker but seemingly a man who had an air of authority and exercised it freely, for, when he heard that thieves had broken into Adams' cottage, he made his way there. When subsequently he found Adams dying, he demanded if any enquiries had been set in motion regarding the culprits. He was told that they were more concerned about the old man.

When John Adams showed him the pistol he had found, Heatherley promptly took charge of it and rode into Walsall, where he handed the weapon over to John Raymond, the town's superintendent of police. This officer knew his patch and most of its rogues, and his suspicion quickly fell on Thomas Boswell, possibly because he was already in trouble with the law.

An application to the Government for a £100 reward upon conviction of the offender(s) was made, a fact which was to play an important part when Boswell gave evidence at the trial.

This done, Raymond lost no time in making his way to Boswell's house with another officer, whom he wisely placed at the back of the premises whilst he entered at the front. Boswell made an appearance, doubtless quaking in his shoes, and was asked by the superintendent if the pistol was his property. Naturally, he denied having set eyes on it, but he admitted that he had a pistol and obligingly fetched it and gave it to the officer.

The possession of such weapons should not be seen as unusual in that day and age, particularly in that locality, for Wednesbury and, to a greater extent, neighbouring Darlaston were major centres of the gun-making industry, so that it would not be too difficult to obtain firearms.

The extraordinary feature of this case was that Boswell had gone to Adams' cottage armed with a pistol, had not used it, yet was arrested along with his companions because of it.

With Boswell safely locked up, Superintendent Raymond sat down to examine the pistol found in Adams' pantry. In fact, he took it to pieces and, almost as if he knew his efforts would be rewarded, found that it had been repaired to the extent of having had a new mainspring fitted. He had only to find the repairer and get him to identify Boswell as having brought in the weapon for repair, and his case was complete, at least against Boswell.

And that is precisely what he did. He made the rounds of local workshops and eventually located a gun-lock filer named Walter Baggott who said that the pistol he was shown had had a new mainspring fitted by him. It had been brought in by a boy about a month previously, and Boswell had collected it, paying 6d. for the repair. The boy turned out to be sixteen-year-old William Jones of Walsall, who later confirmed that Boswell had given him the pistol and told him to take it to Baggott for repair.

Thus Thomas was safely in the net and, as so often happens with small-time crooks brooding on their plight overnight in a cell, he intimated to Superintendent Raymond on 10 December that he wanted to say something to him in private. Raymond agreed, but only if another officer was present.

Boswell said he had nothing to do with the murder of Adams and that the person who had done the deed was named Joseph Wilkes. Joseph Wilkes, his brother James Wilkes and himself were the only ones to have entered Adams' cottage. He 'grassed' freely, giving accurate descriptions of his associates and saying where they lived. They had firearms, he warned, and would use them.

The superintendent and other officers went to the address at Longacres, Walsall, given them by Boswell and burst the door down. They seized and handcuffed James Wilkes before he could gather his wits, and straight away went off to another house at Shortacres where they found Joseph Wilkes. He was searched and found to have on his person a jemmy and a bunch of skeleton keys. The house he was in was that of a man named John Lingard, and both he and his wife Mary were subsequently to be charged with receiving stolen property – another case entirely.

The next morning the superintendent examined Joseph's jacket and found marks of blood.

Now the baker Samuel Heatherley reappears in the story. How he came to have access to prisoners inside the police station, or police house more likely, is something of a mystery, but he had, and it was to him that Boswell once more proceeded to unburden himself.

'Boswell told me of his own free will,' Heatherley recounted, 'that the superintendent had already got another man in custody who was connected with the attempted robbery at Adams' – George Giles.' He also admitted that the pistol found in Adams' pantry was his, but the other, the one he had shown to the superintendent, belonged to Joseph Wilkes.

So there they all were: Thomas Boswell, Joseph and James Wilkes and George Giles.

The inquest on Matthew Adams had taken place at the Bulls Head, Tame Bridge, on the day before Boswell's revelations to Heatherley, and had consisted solely of viewing the body, being adjourned to the following Monday, this time at the Red Lion in Wednesbury.

There, the case against the prisoners was outlined and the surgeon Thomas Pitt described how he had found two wounds on the left side of the deceased's head, both causing fractures of the skull.

Boswell said that he and his companions had been in Adams' pantry for half an hour and had put out their candles when they heard Adams coming down the stairs. After Joseph Wilkes had hit Adams, James Wilkes had said, 'Come on, or we shall all be taken.' They left in a hurry, and as they fled Boswell told them, 'We shall be taken. I've lost my pistol.'

It was revealed that on 3 December a police officer named Humphries had been asked by Boswell if there was an advertisement out concerning the murder of Adams (he meant the offer of a reward) and was told not yet, but there would be. Boswell asked to have a copy when available, and in due course the officer gave him two copies. It is easy to see how Boswell's cunning mind was working, for after all it was not he who had killed Adams.

His known attitude of looking after number one was feared by the others, as was evident when one John Pearson gave evidence that on the Friday after the murder he had passed the house of the Wilkes brothers' father. James had come out and they had discussed the murder, the former telling Pearson that he was afraid Boswell would confess everything. James told him that after the murder he and Boswell had gone back to look for the pistol but were scared away by the presence of other people.

A further interesting sidelight on the criminal activities of the group under arrest was revealed by another witness, Joseph Smith, a springhook-maker, who lived at Walsall. On the Sunday morning before the crime (28 November), he had met Boswell in Walsall, and the latter had said, 'You are just the man I am looking for ... I have heard where there is a good booty.' He then told Smith about the £100 that Adams was said to have in hand to present to his granddaughter. 'You come to my workshop at eight o'clock tomorrow night. I have a brace of pistols.' He added that there he would meet Giles and two others who would accompany them to Adams' cottage.

Luckily for Smith, he did not promise to go. Later on in the morning of the murder he again met Boswell in Walsall and was told that he was a 'faint-hearted fellow'. Boswell then said, 'We went and cracked that crib, but I did not get a bloody shilling. I hope you won't say anything but I think we have settled the old man.'

So all along one sees that Boswell was the ringleader, gathering a band of criminals together, perhaps not for the first time. Joseph Smith's slate was by no means clean, and doubtless it was only chance that had kept him in the clear on this occasion.

What did not seem to have occurred to any of the miscreants was the fact that Adams might not have the money in the house. Ironically, it transpired that Adams had already handed over the money to his granddaughter.

The jury returned a verdict of wilful murder against Joseph Wilkes as principal, in the first degree, and against James Wilkes, Thomas Boswell and George Giles, as principals in the second degree, and they were committed for trial at the Spring Assizes in the following year.

What happened after the inquest has about it an element of farce, certainly from the standpoint of today.

All the prisoners, along with John Wilkes, father of Joseph and James, set off to the Walsall lock-up in a cart, accompanied by several police officers, Superintendent Raymond and his wife, together with the baker Heatherley. Wilkes senior was in custody on another charge, and as the cart lumbered slowly along, the occupants chatted, and chatted and chatted.

Charlotte Raymond (what was she doing there?) said later that John Wilkes and his son Joseph had talked freely about the murder and she had commented to Joseph, 'Your old man has brought you to this.' Joseph had replied, 'He knows nothing about it. The man is in this cart that told such tales [Boswell] or I should never have gone to Adams' place.'

Mrs Raymond then asked: 'How came you to kill him?'

Joseph answered, regardless of the police presence, 'I don't know. It doesn't matter now. It was me that killed him. I struck him. He had a pike in his hand and I thought he was going to run me through with it.'

Giles put in his two-pennyworth, telling the superintendent that it was the first robbery he had been in. 'If you had not come for me as you did, I should have sold the cow and been on the road to America by now.' Here is an inconsistency, since Boswell had told Heatherley that Giles was already in custody. Truth was seemingly at a premium.

All such conversations were duly noted by Superintendent Raymond.

The eventful year of 1842 dawned, a year in which the British garrison of Kabul was wiped out during the Afghan War, with the loss of some 15,000 lives; of the so-called 'Opium Wars' in China and, on a more pleasurable note, of the conclusion of a European treaty for the more effective suppression of the slave trade.

Against such momentous happenings, immediate or pending, the trial of a sordid bunch of criminals tinged with the 'gloss' of murder nevertheless attracted widespread attention; the court was filled and there was uproar when vast numbers could not be admitted to the Stafford courtroom on Wednesday 9 March.

The case was heard by Mr Justice Creswell (1794-1863, MP for Liverpool 1837-41), Mr Lee and Mr Whitemore prosecuting and Mr Yardley defending Boswell and Giles. The Wilkes brothers were undefended.

After outlining the gravity of the case, Lee called the same witnesses who had appeared at the inquest. Samuel Heatherley, who always seemed to know more than anyone else, told how he had visited Boswell at the police station and had had several conversations with him. These were at first received as evidence by the judge, but when Heatherley related how Boswell had been given printed hand-bills stating that a reward was offered by the Government for the discovery of the murderer and, on the impeachment of an accomplice, if not the actual murderer, the offer of Her Majesty's pardon, he changed his mind. The whole of the conversations between Boswell and Heatherley were struck out, as there was reason to believe that they had been made by Boswell in the hope of obtaining the benefit of the Government offer.

Cheeky Boswell: hoping to get paid for a crime he had organized!

Mrs Raymond gave evidence, having been present in the cart. (Is that how the expression 'in the cart' arises?) She recounted her conversation with Joseph Wilkes, and then Samuel Heatherley came to the stand and said that whilst in the cart he had asked Joseph Wilkes if it was a cosh with which he had killed Adams. Wilkes had replied that he did not know what it was, having thrown it away in a field as they fled.

Heatherley then told how he had spoken to Giles in gaol. Giles had said, 'You know we are badly off. I hope you will call on my uncle John and ask him to do something for me.' It was, Giles said, better to get transportation for seven years than for life.

So he anticipated seven years, yet he had acted only as look-out!

A new witness, Eli Shelton, a blacksmith who lived near Matthew Adams, said he knew that the hammer used to strike the fatal blows had belonged to the deceased. Some days before his death, Adams had asked him to lend him a heavier one. It was Shelton who had found the hammer thrown away by Joseph Wilkes. It was lying in a field about a hundred yards from Adams' cottage, and it had grey hairs upon it.

Joseph Smith's evidence that he had been approached by Boswell to take part in the burglary was challenged by the defence on the grounds that, since he had previously been charged with highway robbery and stealing a hat, his account of events was not to be relied upon.

After the surgeon Thomas Pitt had described the head wounds sustained by Adams, and agreed that the hammer produced in court *might* have caused the fracture to the skull which had resulted in death, the case for the prosecution was concluded, and the jury retired for refreshment.

On the resumption of the case, Mr Yardley addressed the jury on behalf of Boswell and Giles, begging them to consider the case of these men separately '... because the facts affecting them were quite different'. He said that he objected to the declaration made by Boswell because it was the rule of law and of common sense to exclude what might be said of a prisoner under the circumstances in which the declarations were made by Boswell. In other words, Boswell would have done better to have kept his mouth shut, instead of blabbing in the hope of receiving a reward.

'He was bound to say,' Yardley continued, 'that the case against Boswell gave him more anxiety than that against Giles. There was not a tittle of evidence to show that Giles had any hand in the death of Adams ... the only evidence against him being the conversation in the cart on returning from the inquest.' Yardley went on to cite a previous case to make the point that it was dangerous to rely on the 'conversations of parties'.

His plea on Boswell's behalf consisted mainly in discrediting the evidence of Smith, who had been approached to take part in the burglary. 'Having on his own evidence heard of the proposed robbery,' said Yardley, 'he had taken no steps to prevent it. Bearing in mind the man's character, it suggested that Smith had made up the story in the hope of obtaining a portion of the reward. Beside, he had an old grudge against Boswell which he might now be seeking to pay off.'

Now came the summing-up, the judge telling the jury that it would be for them to consider for what purpose the party had gone to Adams' house. 'If they went out armed, and were determined to offer such resistance as might lead to the death of an opposing party, even though that death were the act of one of the party, yet they would all be equally guilty. It was not necessary that all should have been present when the blow was struck.'

With such firm guidelines, it took the jury only ten minutes to reach a verdict: Joseph Wilkes guilty of murder but, surprisingly, going against the judge's edict, the other three prisoners not guilty of murder. In fact, acquitted.

Joseph Wilkes was aged seventeen and 'probably younger', the youngest of the prisoners, which is why in passing sentence the judge lectured him on having fallen into evil company (a side-swipe at the others) leading on to evil ways. 'Your earthly trial is over ... beware of the more awful tribunal beyond the grave.'

Mr Justice Creswell then sentenced Wilkes to death, a particularly stressful ordeal for him personally, since it was the first time he had been called upon to perform this duty. Observers noted that, after Wilkes was removed from the dock, the judge leaned back and hid his face in his hand, obviously distressed.

An appeal was set up backed by 'influential persons' in an attempt to obtain a remission of the sentence on the grounds of the youth of the prisoner and the fact that he had taken no deadly weapon with him to the house – he may not have known that Boswell had a pistol – and that the blows he had rained on Adams with a hammer picked up on the premises were unpremeditated. Moreover, he was acting under the influence and instructions of those older and in reality more guilty than himself.

The reasoning here was weighty and valid, but the Home Secretary, Sir James Graham, turned down the appeal, and Joseph Wilkes was executed publicly on 2 April 1842. After the 'drop' he was seen to struggle for some time and '... appeared to die with difficulty'.

But that was not the end of the story, for, on the day following their trial for murder, James Wilkes, Thomas Boswell and George Giles were again in court, this time charged with '...burglariously breaking and entering the house of Matthew Adams with intent to commit a felony'.

Mr Lees and Mr Whitemore prosecuted, but on this occasion Mr Yardley acted solely on behalf of Giles. The same witnesses were laboriously examined over again, and it boiled down to verdicts of guilty against all three men, Giles being recommended to mercy. James Wilkes and Thomas Boswell were sentenced to transportation for the terms of their natural lives, and George Giles for seven years.

At these same Spring Assizes fifty-year-old James Wilkes, father of Joseph and James, was tried for a burglary committed in North Staffordshire, along with John and Mary Lingard for receiving stolen property. (It will be remembered that Joseph Wilkes had been taken into custody at the Lingards' house). All three were found not guilty.

As to the transportation of the three men, this was to prove no salvation for two of them. All three sailed for Van Diemen's Land on the *Waterloo*, but it sank off the Cape of

Good Hope with the loss of most of the convicts herded aboard. Boswell and Giles were drowned. Only James Wilkes survived to reach Van Diemen's Land safely.

In 1853 the Transportation Act was partially abolished, penal servitude being substituted unless the sentence was for fourteen years or more. Four years later transportation was abolished altogether.

One cannot but marvel at the lax attitude of the police in allowing people unconnected with the crime to ride in the cart conveying the prisoners, let alone converse with them in the lock-up. However, it has to be taken in the context of the time, for the first 'New Police' force in the Black Country, consisting of paid, uniformed officers, came into being at Walsall only in 1835, under the Municipal Corporation Act – Walsall then being the only Black Country borough. During 1841 the Walsall force had only three officers, and Superintendent Raymond was thus one of the first – perhaps *the* first – of the 'New Police' in Britain to arrest a murderer. In fact, he was commended by Mr Justice Creswell for his smart work.

It was surely Thomas Boswell who was the real culprit. He was the ringleader who had set up the burglary and he who, in Adams' pantry, had sent young Joseph Wilkes round to the front door. Doubtless the lad had wished to appear the 'tough guy' in the eyes of his mates.

4   Two Killings Among Nailers, Quarry Bank and Lye, 1856

Nowhere in the Black Country was the plight of the working men, women and children more desperate than that of the thousands employed in the nail trade during the middle of the nineteenth century. Whole families, including children as young as seven years of age, worked in backyard nail shops, usually adjoining their homes, slaving from morn till night to eke out a meagre and miserable existence.

It had been different in the previous century and earlier, when a nailer could profitably combine his trade with agriculture or some other pursuit, but with the advent of machine-cut nails in the 1830s it became a cut-throat trade.

One finds it difficult in these days of sophisticated fastening devices to appreciate the world-wide dependence on the humble nail, but to take just one example, prior to 1830 the East India Dock Company had bought 110 tons of hand-made nails annually for tea chests – six years later, all were made by machine.

Luckily the variety of nails made for different purposes ran into hundreds, and the new machines could not yet cope with the horseshoe nail, whose head was bent over onto the top of the hoof to secure it in place, this being cut when the nail was withdrawn to remove the shoe. Reliability was essential, for, should the nail break off in the hoof, it caused trouble for both horse and blacksmith.

Considering that the horse was the predominant mode of transport of the time, it might be thought that those engaged in horse-nail making still had a future, and so they might have had but for the wickedness of the middle-man, or 'fogger', who stood between them and the merchants. Generally himself a former nail-maker, the fogger had no compunction in cheating by using false weights when supplying nailers with the necessary iron rods, and again when buying back the finished nails, thereby robbing those who depended upon him twice at every deal.

Nor was that all. Despite the Truck Act of 1831, which made it illegal for foggers to pay for finished nails with tokens which nailers could spend in their 'tommy shops' and beer-houses (which supplied inferior goods at prices higher than those elsewhere), the practice did not die out for several decades.

Add to this that the trade became increasingly female orientated, both sexes working in cramped conditions side by side in near nakedness by reason of the constant heat of the forge, and it is hardly surprising that immorality, drunkenness and violence were facts of everyday life.

This was the background against which the killings in this story took place, in adjacent localities close to the market town of Stourbridge.

Case No. 1

Fifteen-year-old Thomas Brown had been out with his parents on the evening of 9 March 1856. We do not know where they had been – perhaps to visit distant relatives – but it was about 3.30 in the morning when they reached Quarry Bank, having probably walked many miles, as was imperative if the poor were to go anywhere. Anyhow, here they were in the dark and fog, with visibility about three yards, and either Thomas was walking ahead after the manner of eager youth or his eyesight was sharper, for he spotted the body of a man lying in the road. 'I did not speak to him,' he said later. 'I walked to him and took his hand. It was cold.'

His parents promptly sent him to the nearby New Inn public house to knock up the landlord, but the latter told the lad to tell the police. So Thomas went to Brierley Hill police station and returned with an officer named Middleton who immediately recognized the deceased as David Taylor, whom he knew well and who had lived with his father at Quarry Bank. Moreover, he recalled having seen Taylor on that Sunday afternoon in company with Joseph Raybold, Samuel Grosvenor and two others whom he did not know. They were then all sober.

'I got a light,' Middleton told the inquest on the following Wednesday, 'held it close and discovered a wound in the deceased's chest and various cuts to his face. There was blood on his clothing and on the ground, and there were signs that a scuffle had taken place.'

There had indeed been a scuffle, and after Taylor was stabbed, guilty and innocent alike all ran away leaving the body in the road for young Brown to find hours later.

It transpired that there had been an affray which had arisen in the first place through what in the Black Country would be termed 'gaming' – larking about. A gang of youths, mainly horse-nail-makers, including the deceased, had come down the High Street at some time between midnight and one o'clock and, just as today youngsters will push supermarket trolleys down steps and wedge them in lifts, so these lads spotted a hand-cart outside a house and decided to have fun with it. One of them grabbed it by the shafts and ran it against the door of the family to whom it belonged, by name Chivers.

Then the trouble started. Joseph Chivers and his brother Josiah ran from their house in a rage, and the whole thing rapidly got out of hand – with fatal results; such were the tensions and traumas of the times that this small prank was too much.

Joseph Morris, describing himself as a foreman living at Mount Pleasant, Quarry Bank (such poor areas often bore incongruously pretty names!), told how he knew the deceased and had seen him at about 12.30 on the Sunday night (Monday morning) standing in the road in company with Samuel Grosvenor, William Bangham, Joseph Raybold, Herbert Foxhall, Joseph Chivers and his brother Josiah. Joseph Chivers was in a threatening mood and accused Taylor of having run the cart against his door. Taylor denied having done so, and all his mates declared that they had not meddled with the cart either.

A fight ensued and, according to Morris, the Chivers' father came out of the house and joined in. 'My wife, my daughter, as well as myself, saw that someone was down,' Morris went on. 'I couldn't see who it was, but then two women came up and one said, "Follow them and give them some more" whereupon Joseph Chivers ran to Taylor and knocked him down. When he was on the ground Taylor cried out "murder" and Joseph Chivers said to him "You … I'll murder you!" '

Morris said that Joseph was 'on him' for four or five minutes. 'As soon as Chivers left Taylor I moved away and saw no more of him. The others all ran away. I saw the Chivers enter their house. I did not speak to them and saw nothing in Joseph Chivers' hand.'

Joseph Raybold then gave evidence and told how he and his mates had left Stourbridge at a quarter to eleven and walked to Quarry Bank (it seems to have taken them a remarkably long time to get there).

'Joseph Chivers came out of his house and collared me, saying I was the one who had knocked his cart against the door. I said I hadn't and he called me a liar. So I told him to ask the others, then he knocked me down. He said "I'll knock your brains out" and I yelled out. Taylor and Bangham came up and got Chivers off me. Then he started on them … I was so badly hurt I could hardly move. I saw Chivers knock Taylor down, and I should say he was on him for five minutes before he got off and joined his father and brother.

'I heard Chivers' mother say, "I fear you have killed him,

Joe", and her son answered, "If I have not, I will." '

Samuel Grosvenor then told how he had seen Joseph Chivers accuse Raybold of meddling with the cart, then attack him and knock him down. 'He then knocked me down, and when I told him I should report him to the police, he knocked me out. When I came to I went home.'

Herbert Foxall then gave his version. He was now a chain-maker – many nail-makers turned to chain as the nail trade went into decline, for the premises and equipment needed were similar. He had seen the cart in the road, and Taylor had been the one to pick it up. 'We all ran down the road and Joseph Chivers and his brothers came after us. He overtook Raybold first.'

Who had hit whom and when was more confusing, but all agreed that it was indeed Joseph Chivers who had got Taylor pinned to the ground.

Thomas Bloomer, another horse-nail-maker, lived opposite to where the affray took place. He had been in bed with his wife, and she had awoken him to say there was a disturbance outside and someone crying 'murder'. 'I opened the window and asked what was the matter. No one answered, but I heard a scuffle and fighting. I recognized Chivers by his voice as he uttered threats, and I also heard a woman say, "Yes, it is our Joe. He has his wife confined and they have been running the cart against the door." '

Bloomer said it was so foggy that he could not pick out any particular person and did not know that anyone was murdered.

The post-mortem on Taylor was carried out by Mr Norris, a surgeon at Brierley Hill, who described the fatal wound in medical terms which few of his listeners would have made head or tail of. In short, a lung had been pierced and the heart penetrated. 'Death,' he said, 'was instantaneous.'

Joseph Chivers was brought before the magistrates on 20 March at Wordsley Police Office, along with his brother

Josiah, his father, Josiah senior, and, surprisingly, Mary Chivers, wife of Josiah senior, and Lavinia, the wife of Josiah Chivers junior. They were all charged with wilful murder.

Superintendent Mills, who with PC Millington had arrested Joseph Chivers, told how the prisoner had remarked that it was the first time he had been taken by *two* police officers – rather as if there were merit in it. On the way to the lock-up Joseph had said, 'I'm sorry the man is dead, but I never struck a blow.'

Joseph Morris repeated his evidence, which was treated as being of major importance, since he had not been one of the gang involved in the affray. He added, sensibly, that he had not interfered because his wife and daughter had urged him not to do so. They were not called.

All other evidence given was as before, and at the end the defence lawyer, Mr Burbery, said that, 'Appearing as he did in a charge of such grave nature, and feeling that the magistrates would probably commit Joseph Chivers to take trial, it became him to be cautious as to how he compared the evidence of the various witnesses. There was no kind of evidence against either of the Josiah Chivers or against the two women. The main evidence was that of Morris, who seemed to say that no others charged had any connection with the affray *after* Taylor had fallen to the ground. If they had no concern in the affray after that period of time, they could no more be implicated in this charge than any of the other persons who Morris said were fighting at the time he arrived on the spot.'

Burbery went on at some length, concluding by declaring that there was no evidence against any person '... except as it might be Joseph Chivers'.

After consultation, the chairman of the bench discharged the two women with a caution not to egg their menfolk into violence, and then discharged the Josiah Chivers, father and son.

Joseph was committed for trial at Stafford Assizes. As he was taken away, the road from Wordsley to Brierley Hill was lined with spectators anxious to see this man who had turned a common scrap into a murder. Most of the men assembled could at one time or another in their lives have so easily found themselves in a similar situation in this slum-ridden, slave-driving society, still in the dying years of the region's Industrial Revolution heyday.

Joseph Chivers stood trial on 21 July before Mr Justice Wightman (1784-1863). Mr Best and Mr Byrne prosecuted; Mr Huddleston and Mr Motteram defended. Huddleston did his best by dwelling on the fact that the prisoner's wife was near her confinement on the night in question and that the conduct of the deceased and his companions had tended to alarm and distress her. 'As a result her husband had interposed, a scuffle had taken place, and the deceased unfortunately came by his death in the struggle. Several respectable witnesses had given the accused a good character.'

His painting a picture of a happy household awaiting an addition to the family and being plagued by a gang of mischievous youths must have struck home, for after his lordship had summed up, the jury returned a verdict of manslaughter.

His lordship did not appear to be over-pleased and said that, whilst the jury had mercifully considered that there was no premeditated malice, it was nevertheless a most serious offence. 'There could,' he said, 'be no doubt that the wounds inflicted had occurred after the cause of the provocation had ceased. The case was in fact very little short of murder, and the sentence would therefore be fifteen years transportation.'

It may be noted that no mention was made of Chivers' having used a knife or other sharp weapon on Taylor. One would have thought that would have weighed heavily against him.

However, fifteen years on the far side of the world, and a wife with a new-born babe! Was it harsh that no account was taken of this? Well, he *had* killed a man.

But wait. Consider …

Case No. 2 (concluded at these same assizes)
> When I entered the village, amazed I stood
> To see all the houses and shops built with mud.
> And as I walked forward I could but admire
> The young damsels, half-naked, were hammering fire.
>
> Men, women and children were making nails;
> They were cheerfully singing and telling droll tales.
> Jolly Bacchus, their god, and him only they fear,
> For wherever they pray it's for ale or strong beer.

'Cheerful'? Well, not always; but thus the Lye Waste, described in verse long after the year 1856 with which we are concerned here. It was 'the last place God ever made', a 'waste' (meaning a no-man's land) settled at first by what one would now call squatters. It did not boast a chapel of any kind until 1806 when the Unitarians came along, and the 'ale and strong beer' reference derives from the fact that there were some fifty-five pubs or beer-houses to about 6,000 inhabitants.

The early dwellings and shops (meaning nail shops) built by inhabitants, had walls of straw and mud composition, thatched roofs and floors of local clay. One such dwelling was found as recently as 1956, disguised by an outer layer of brick added at some later date.

Mindless vandalism? Who says it is new? At around the time the killing we are about to consider took place, someone smashed down the door of a house where an old lady lay in her coffin. The corpse was thrown onto a bed, the coffin taken to an old pit-shaft and thrown down it. Later it was seen floating on water in the shaft, whereupon it was retrieved and repaired, the corpse replaced inside, and burial arranged that same day before further mischief could befall.

Having set the grim scene of the times, let us focus on a particular nail shop on the afternoon of 27 June 1856. It is hot, the work is tediously repetitive, and the hours are long. By the middle of the afternoon, tempers, seldom far from the surface, are beginning to smoulder.

Horse nails were being made. On one side of the hearth stood twenty-two-year-old John Phipson, whilst opposite, on the far side of the hearth, a distance of two yards, was Elizabeth Millward. Both were single. The nail shop belonged to Phipson's brother, who was absent at the time.

Also at work in the shop was Elizabeth's illegitimate daughter Eliza, aged about eighteen, and a ten-year-old-girl named Mary Ann, who was John Phipson's niece. All were hard at work when Elizabeth Millward passed a jug of water to her daughter. After taking a drink, Eliza handed the jug to the young girl Mary Ann, who also had a drink and then passed the jug to her uncle – a fatal mistake!

It seems ludicrous that serious trouble could flare up over such a commodity as water, but, of course, there was no simple turning of a tap in those days: it had to be fetched, probably from a well, and Elizabeth Millward, who was about forty-eight years of age and doubtless not above exerting her seniority, did not see why John Phipson should drink from her jug.

Quite possibly there had been trouble over this before. Anyhow, in a fury Elizabeth threw a handful of slack across the hearth into John's face. He threw some back, and she promptly threw some more, increasingly angry. It was not ordinary coal slack but the tiny shards from the hammering of countless nails, and it was sharp to the skin.

John Phipson had had enough. He drew from the hearth the red-hot bar on which he was working and flung it at Elizabeth, point first. It pierced her side, and she fell screaming across her anvil. The iron fell out of her body.

Eliza, bent as usual over her work, did not see the

incident but heard her mother scream and ran to her *after finishing her nail* – such was the discipline of the trade. Hearing the scream, Elizabeth Pool, who was working in her own nail shop 'about three yards away', ran next door and found Eliza holding her mother as she leaned across the anvil. 'She screamed twice after I got to her,' Pool said later.

Another worker, Ann Wood, also came in and together they got the injured woman into the back yard. Elizabeth Pool fetched a can of water and gave it to Mrs Wood to try to revive Mrs Millward, whilst she went back to John Phipson, who was still at his stall.

Ann Wood attempted to put water into Mrs Millward's mouth, but she gave a gasp and died. She lived only three or four minutes after leaving the nail shop.

The parish constable, Josiah Brooke, was sent for and found Phipson in his house. As he subsequently told the court, 'I said to him that it was a very serious thing he had done and I would have to take him to the lock-up. He washed himself and changed his clothes, then said, "I was drinking some water and she threw slack at me, and I returned it. I had an iron in my hand. She leaned back and it went into her." '

The hearing took place the next day at the Public Office, Stourbridge, Mr Burbery defending. It was said that Mrs Millward was deaf and had a violent temper, yet when Eliza Millward was questioned about their relationship at work, she said that they were all friends together. Mrs Wood told how she had gone to John Phipson after Mrs Millward had died and pointed to the iron, saying, 'Is that what you hit her with?' and he had told her, 'It has not hurt her, I hope'; he had '… looked as if he was going to drop'.

Mr Harding, a surgeon, said that he had examined the body and found a penetrating wound in the thorax on the left side, entering between the ninth and tenth ribs and passing in an upward direction towards the spine, inflicting a wound and burn of the left bronchus and case of the left lung, and a large irregular wound of the aorta. Death was caused by loss of blood from the wound of the aorta. 'I think the iron must have been thrown with considerable force, seeing that it penetrated more than four inches from the skin. I should think the iron was white hot.'

John Phipson made no reply to questions, and Mr Burbery asked the bench to commit on the minor charge of manslaughter. However, after consideration, his plea was discarded and Phipson was charged with wilful murder.

That same afternoon the inquest was held at the Holly Bush inn, and again Mr Burbery appealed on behalf of Phipson, who had by this time been taken to gaol. All the evidence was heard anew, without deviation, but the result was different, for the jury returned a verdict of manslaughter.

Now to the Stafford Assizes, Mr Best prosecuting, Mr Powell defending. Eliza Millward was asked by Mr Justice Wightman if her mother had thrown the slack at Phipson in fun or to hurt him. Eliza replied that she was angry at the time, but she did not know what about. Elizabeth Pool took the stand and said that the slack, being the 'beatings' from the iron nails, would give great pain if it got into the eyes. Was she trying to justify Phipson's act as a spontaneous response to pain? Whether she was or not, as the case proceeded things began to look decidedly more hopeful for the prisoner.

After the surgeon had given his evidence concerning the injuries inflicted upon the deceased, the judge said to him, 'It was a singular act then?', to which the surgeon replied that it was and that the degree of injury could not have been expected. That was the clincher, the inference being that one could throw any number of similar hot iron bars at a person and not do the fatal damage that this one had. Thus, when his lordship addressed the jury, he told them they could not find the prisoner guilty of wilful murder but only of manslaughter.

Mr Powell, defending, said that the only reasonable defence he could offer was that the prisoner, blinded by the slack thrown by the deceased, was going to take up some to return it and accidentally took up the piece of iron with the handful of slack and threw it, not knowing that it was in his hand. It was a ridiculous assumption, and quite unnecessary in view of the judge's remarks to the jury.

The jury having returned a verdict of manslaughter as directed, the judge addressed John Phipson, pointing out the ill-effects sometimes resulting from a momentary yielding to passion. He would, he said, pass but a light sentence, which would be a fortnight's solitary imprisonment.

So there you have it: two killings both impulsive rather than premeditated. One man gets fifteen years transportation whilst the other escapes with just two weeks solitary.

At that same assizes an eighteen-year-old girl received twelve months imprisonment for stealing two loaves of bread and a 'quantity' of butter, taken, no doubt, to ward off starvation rather than for monetary gain.

In the year that saw the end of the Crimean War, sentencing was as inconsistent as it sometimes appears to be today.

5 The Clue of the Hand-Made Fishing-Bag, Dudley, 1957

1957 was a momentous year for Britain and for the world. In March the Treaty of Rome was signed by the original six member states, so creating the European Economic Community; the British tested an hydrogen bomb early that summer, and on 4 October the Russians launched Sputnik 1, which circled the world every ninety-five minutes. The space-age had begun.

There was also a sterling crisis in Harold Macmillan's never-had-it-so-good premiership when, in September, devaluationary measures sent the bank rate up to an unheard-of seven per cent.

The year was also an important one for Dudley: the Queen and Prince Philip were to visit the town, the first visit by a reigning sovereign for over 400 years, except for the unheralded appearance of George VI and his queen under the wartime security of 1942. The event took place on a gloriously hot day, 23 April, Easter Tuesday, and the town was *en fête.*

It was also an important year for Detective Inspector Fishwick, who was responsible during the royal visit for co-ordinating the disposition of police officers from several surrounding forces. Shortly afterwards he handed in his resignation after twenty-five years police service, little knowing that, even as his notice lay on the chief constable's desk, he was to become involved in one of the most exhaustive cases of his career, the murder of a Dudley shopkeeper.

Wolverhampton Street, Dudley, actually does lead to

Wolverhampton, branching off the main High Street, an age-old shopping street but never a site for high-class shops or stores. No. 21 was Halfords, a men's outfitters shop run as a partnership by Mr David Keasey and his twenty-one-year-old son, David Alan. On the late afternoon of Friday 17 May young David was looking after the shop when a man came in with intent to rob. David resisted and was shot at close range. As the assailant ran into the street, he shouted to passersby, 'Someone has had a fit.' As he ran, he added, 'I'll fetch a doctor' – or 'Fetch a doctor', no one was sure of the exact words. The man quickly disappeared towards the centre of the town, mingling with the shoppers.

Several people were close to the shop. One declared he had heard a scream and a sound like breaking glass; another said that the man rushing out of the shop had almost brushed his clothes. A third man, a gas-fitter, said he had looked into the shop and seen a man lying on his back with his head towards the counter. He entered and removed the man's collar, tie and part of his shirt. Keasey was gasping but did not speak. There was fluster and confusion around the doorway.

Particularly harrowing, as it turned out, was the fact that, it being near to closing time, David Keasey's fiancée arrived within minutes from her own place of work in order to meet him. She was horrified to find Alan, as she called him, lying on the floor and being attended to by a stranger. An ambulance arrived and she accompanied her fiancé to the Guest Hospital, where ironically she was employed and which she had left only shortly before. Before getting into the ambulance she had the presence of mind to put down the catch on the shop door and close it, noticing at a glance that the till drawer was closed.

Young Keasey was found dead on arrival at the hospital, where a cursory examination revealed no evidence of murder. He was thought to have died of a heart attack, and his body was removed to the mortuary.

Now Detective Inspector Walter ('Wally') Fishwick comes into the story. I was fortunate in being able to visit him and hear his own account of the investigation.

'I had been on duty and was going home to tea at six o'clock, calling at a house on the way in connection with some routine inquiry. An officer caught up with me in a police car with a message to go at once to the Guest Hospital. It was from the matron, whom I knew well, and when I got there and saw Keasey lying undressed in the mortuary, she showed me a tiny hole under the deceased's left shoulder blade.

'Having been trained in firearms, I realized that the hole was the size of a .25 bullet. There were no powder burns, so I asked for his clothing and, sure enough, found a hole through the jacket, shirt and vest. There was no exit wound, and the jacket was not even singed, indicating that the gun had been pressed right into the cloth.'

Fishwick knew he had a murder on his hands and ordered police officers to guard the front and rear of the shop. 'I expected to find a brass cartridge-case and wanted everything protected until I got there, which was about eight-o'clock that evening. I went in with another officer, and we immediately found a box as big as a cigarette packet. I breathed on it, and a thumbprint appeared. I had never seen one more perfect. Then I found the cartridge-case on the carpeted floor. There was no sign of a struggle, and no bloodstains.'

The third piece of evidence was the bullet itself, which, when removed from the body, was proved to have been fired from a .25 weapon with a damaged barrel.

Scotland Yard were called in, and Superintendent George Miller and Detective Sergeant Gentle arrived. Intensive enquiries were put in hand, with a number of officers covering the ground. There was no new information, despite loud-speaker appeals throughout the area, and Mr Fishwick told me how he tried all he knew to keep the case alive in the newspapers. For example, one day on his way to an enquiry at Walsall, accompanied by a Scotland Yard man, he came upon a fire at Coseley. Old railway sleepers, a shed and a hedge were ablaze, and he sent for the fire brigade before tackling the fire. Later he organized photographs of himself, his colleagues, the fire chief and a local policeman, and one duly appeared with some such caption as 'On the way to Walsall to investigate outfitter's murder'.

Thus are unsolved crimes sometimes kept in the public eye.

One day Fishwick and the Scotland Yard men were at the YMCA at Wolverhampton when he was called to the phone and heard a friendly finger-print expert in Birmingham say, 'You are a lucky bugger, Wally. You have the fingerprint on that cardboard box which matches that found at George Bates' gunmakers' premises in Steelhouse Lane [Birmingham]. A lot of guns were stolen. We've had no luck with the case at all. Months of deadlock.'

The next break was when a policeman on the Smethwick force phoned Fishwick, saying, 'I don't know if it is of any use to you, but we have heard of young people being seen with firearms.'

By that time the Scotland Yard men had returned to London, but this new information brought them back again, and they learned that the Smethwick police had knowledge of a person with a lot of firearms.

It transpired that it was an ex-Borstal boy who had seen young lads with guns, and they had told him they used them when committing a crime. Fishwick and the Yard men obtained a list of the weapons stolen from the gun shop, and they decided to seek out and talk to these youngsters.

'They were frightened to death,' Fishwick recalled. 'One kid admitted he had had a weapon which he kept hidden in a wardrobe. His Dad had found it and told him to throw it in the canal. I took a very dim view of that particular parent's action.'

Fishwick persevered with this lad, asking a question which seemed irrelevant, but only because he had a trick up his sleeve. Some time before, he had visited the gun shop in Birmingham and talked with the manager. He had asked what the manager thought the thief had used to carry the stolen weapons away in, and was told that it was a green fishing-bag. He was shown one like it. They were special, hand-made at Walsall. Thinking it might be useful, Fishwick borrowed the bag he was shown. He was now on the point of getting his man.

'What,' he enquired of the lad, 'did the person who lent you the gun keep it in? You've been with him; you must know.'

One can only imagine the inspector's elation when the lad told him, 'A bag. He used to let me have it to go fishing.'

Concealing his excitement, the inspector spoke to the lad gently: 'Look! You don't want to get into trouble. You help me with the fishing-bag, and I will help you.'

So it was arranged that the lad should go to where he knew the person lived and ask to borrow the bag to go fishing, a constable being detailed to hide round a corner. The ruse worked like a dream. The lad returned with the bag, identical to the one Fishwick had borrowed and obviously the one stolen. The officers knew they were almost at the end of their trail, but so far they did not know the name of the person they were after.

They did not immediately go to the house but learned from one of the youths they were questioning that, this being a Saturday night, the man they sought would be at a 'do' in Birmingham, so they got the Birmingham crime squad to visit dance halls, meanwhile keeping a watch on the house, 3 Lones Road, Smethwick, and sealing off the estate.

Miller and Fishwick went to the door at about 11.20, having seen a man return. It was now 22 June, and over a month of freedom was at an end for Keasey's killer.

'We knocked on the door, and a youth answered,'

Fishwick told me. 'I asked if he was Dennis Howard, for we now had a name. He said, "No, that's my brother," and he shouted upstairs, "Dennis, someone wants to see you." '

As Dennis Howard appeared at the top of the stairs, Miller ran up, put his arms round him and brought him down and out into the front garden. This was a courageous act on Miller's part, for, as they were going in, Fishwick had said, 'You realize we could be shot at?' And so they could, for Howard had loaded weapons in his room.

Miller told him he believed he was in possession of a number of stolen firearms and, if so, he would like to see them. At first Howard blustered that he had no idea what Miller was talking about. 'Weapons? What weapons?' But when Miller told him they wanted to look in his room, he agreed after only slight hesitation, although he could have refused, since they had no search warrant. 'You can come up,' he said, 'but don't make a noise because mother's not well.' In fact, she was dying of cancer.

The officer, joined by Detective Sergeant Gentle, followed Howard into a small front room, and there they found a number of guns, ammunition and textbooks on guns. 'The lad was fanatical about them,' Mr Fishwick recalled. 'Rather like that Hungerford chap' [Michael Ryan, 1987].'

As Fishwick handed Gentle two Smith & Wesson revolvers, Howard said, 'Be careful. Some of them are loaded.' He handed Miller several other weapons, and the officers made a list. They then arrested Howard for a gun-shop break-in.

'As we stood there crowded into that tiny room,' Fishwick said, 'I signified to Howard that there was something involved other than robbery. "You do know what it is?" I put to him. "The Dudley murder," he replied. "That's right," I said. Then I told him that I not only believed he had done it but knew that he had.'

Mr Fishwick told me that, as they brought Howard to Dudley in the car, they passed an ironmonger's shop in

Oldbury. 'Howard pointed to it and said, "That is where I bought the bolt-cutters I used to break into that gun shop. I was going to try and sell them back." '

Dennis Howard appeared before the Dudley magistrates on 10 July, when it was revealed that, in company with another lad, he had been in Dudley with firearms some weeks before the murder but had not committed any crime. One of his many gun-toting companions declared that after the murder Howard had told him, boastfully, that he had shot Keasey. He related how he had seen the clothes shop empty and had gone in to get some money. He drew his gun and asked Keasey to move away from the counter. Instead, Keasey tackled him and they struggled. Then, after warning him twice, he put his arm around Keasey and squeezed the trigger on his gun.

However, having gratuitously given his friend his detailed version of the shooting, Howard then promptly threatened him with what he would do to him, or to anyone else who revealed his secret.

Detective Chief Inspector Albert Ratcliffe, attached to the fingerprint branch of Birmingham City Police, gave evidence that the thumbprint taken at the shop was identical to Howard's right thumbprint: 'On each are sixteen ridge characteristics which are in the same formation and in the same sequence.'

Detective Inspector Fishwick and the two Scotland Yard officers gave evidence of going to 3 Lones Street, Smethwick, finding the weapons and arresting Howard, all details being much the same as Mr Fishwick related to me thirty years later. *No mention of the gun-shop robbery or fishing-bag was introduced.*

Witnesses included David Keasey, the murdered man's father, who stated that he had last seen his son when he left to go to the shop as usual on the morning of 17 May; a woman passerby who said she had heard a scream and a bang which seemed to come from the shop, another woman who said she had seen a man run out of Halfords shop, and the gas-fitter who had gone to Keasey's aid. Then Keasey's fiancée told how she had arrived on the scene and found Alan lying on the floor.

An expert in firearms gave evidence that the bullet which killed Keasey was of .25 inch or 6.35 mm calibre of ICI manufacture. It had been fired through a barrel of six grooves giving a right-hand twist. The cartridge case was of the same calibre and make and had been fired in a self-loading pistol. He then described the considerable amount of weapons and ammunition found in Howard's possession.

Dr Albert Charles Hunt told the court that Keasey had died of a bullet wound to the heart. 'The wound was circular and 5/16 inch in diameter with the entry hole slightly below the centre of the wound.' Internal examination revealed that the bullet had passed slightly downwards and struck the eighth rib, '... and had passed downwards at an angle of forty-five degrees through the chest, puncturing the left lung, aorta, the membrane over the heart, and the right chamber of the heart'. A portion of the flesh and skin had been removed from the wound and was produced in a glass jar as an exhibit. Mr Stephen Brown, counsel for the defence, cross-examined, and Dr Hunt replied that there was no other bruising on the body.

After the accused had been asked if he had anything to say, Brown replied for him: 'He pleads not guilty, and reserves his defence.' Howard was then remanded in custody to await trial at the Worcester Assizes, having been granted legal aid for two counsel.

The trial opened at Worcester on 17 October, presided over by Mr Justice Hinchcliffe QC. Howard was defended by Mr R. G. Micklethwaite QC and Mr Stephen Brown. Following the swearing-in of the jury, the defence asked to make submissions to the judge on certain legal points, and the jury retired for this to be done.

When the case proceeded, Howard, clad in a light blue suit and wearing a mauve tie, spoke in a firm voice as he pleaded not guilty to murdering David Alan Keasey by shooting in furtherance of theft.

Mr Gillespie-Baker, prosecuting, told the jury that this was a charge of capital murder 'of a particularly grave kind'. He explained that 'capital murder' had been carefully defined in a recent Act of Parliament and that, according to that definition, murder by shooting in the furtherance of theft was 'capital'.

Howard was particularly unlucky in his timing. The death sentence had been suspended for two years, for review by Parliament, and had been reintroduced only for certain crimes, including such as his own, in the March prior to his crime in the following May. The death penalty was abolished altogether in 1965.

The prosecution went over the whole story and called the same witnesses as before. When it came to the thumbprint, Mr Baker declared that it was 'left like a visiting-card' just as Detective Inspector Fishwick had realized immediately he spotted it in the shop. Mr Baker told the jury in conclusion: 'If you shoot a man and the pulling of the trigger is a voluntary act and something other than pure accident, and death results, that is murder.'

Giving his version of events, Howard said that he had left home early on the morning of 17 May and had walked to Wolverhampton and then to Dudley – hardly the act of a rational man, since the total distance was all of seventeen miles. He had in his possession a pistol containing three rounds of ammunition. As he passed Keasey's shop late that afternoon, he made up his mind to go in and try to rob the owner of some money. He cocked the gun outside the shop – a statement which must have made his defence counsel and well-wishers wince, for it virtually sealed his fate. Asked by Mr Micklethwaite why he had put the magazine into the pistol before leaving home, Howard said it was to stop the bullets from rolling around in his pocket. No: he could not remember whether the safety catch was on or off.

Howard then tried to make out that he had only meant to frighten '… the fellow behind the counter … I had no intention of firing if the man did not make trouble.' He said that Keasey had run round the counter and tried to get out of the door, which he (Howard) had shut with his foot. 'We struggled … the firing of the gun was accidental. I was in a bit of a panic.'

Questioned by the defence, he said he could not remember telling a friend he had shot Keasey or that he had threatened him if he told the police. All in all, the defence was weak, as indeed it could hardly fail to be, and in the end it came down to Howard's plea that the pistol had been fired unintentionally in the course of a struggle.

The 'unintentional' aspect was negated by his admission of having cocked the gun prior to entering the shop, and after the judge's summing-up, one would have thought that the verdict would have been speedy. In the event, the jury was out for an hour and forty minutes before returning to find Howard guilty.

During the time the jury was out, Mr Fishwick (he had by now retired from the police force) asked if he could see the prisoner, a request granted reluctantly by Howard's custodians, saying, 'You can't stop long.'

Fishwick had come to be accepted by Howard as a friend, strange though that may seem, for during visits to Dudley from Winson Green Prison, whilst on remand, Fishwick had allowed him to sit in his office, and several chats had ensued. Now, as the jury deliberated, some obviously unwilling to pass the fateful verdict and instead give Howard the benefit of any doubts in their mind, Howard told him that he regarded him as a friend and said that the only time he had been happy had been during those informal chats. He had had a miserable life, his mother ill and his brother and sister, so he declared, having nothing to do with him.

'I don't mind paying with my neck,' he said, and as

Fishwick was asked to leave because Howard's solicitor, Stephen Brown, wished to see his client, he shouted after him, 'Wally! Don't say Brown, say Hovis,' quoting a well-known advertisement slogan of the time, and calling him by his nickname.

Even after the lapse of so many years, Mr Fishwick was still touched by this and at the time was sympathetic to the extent of believing that Howard should have been reprieved.

There was an appeal, held on 18 November, but, despite most strenuous effort on Howard's behalf, it failed. Lord Goddard, the Lord Chief Justice – a post he held from 1946 to 1958 – did, however, comment that he thought '... that taking an objection before evidence was tendered was a very inconvenient way of conducting a trial. In civil cases the right time to take an objection was when the evidence was tendered. This was an attempt to get the judge to rule before the evidence was given. The question whether the appellant carried a gun at another time might be relevant or it might not.'

There was considerable discussion along this line, all of which, of course, centred on the robbery Howard had committed to acquire the guns found in his possession. It will be recalled that the jury had been withdrawn from the court and the judge consulted before the trial began, the reason being that Howard's counsel feared that evidence was going to be given of the theft of property and wondered if it was direct evidence at court. If Howard was going to be charged with possessing stolen property, this would disclose another offence with which he was not charged.

Clearly, the defence had not wanted this raised, and Mr Justice Hinchcliffe accepted a submission of Mr Micklethwaite for the defence that certain evidence presented by the prosecution was not admissible: 'Highly prejudiced ... dangerous to admit it ... it would give the jury a false impression.'

So we see that, from start to finish, the robbery at the

Birmingham gun-makers and Detective Inspector Fishwick's all-important fishing-bag were never disclosed, and had I not been able to talk to him in retirement, there would have been a gap in this story as to how Dennis Howard was tracked down.

In point of fact, so strong was the evidence of murder that the police did not arrest him on the lesser charge of robbery, as they could well have done.

The appeal ended with the judge's declaring that there was a very strong case, '... because the appellant admitted that he went into the shop with a cocked pistol, there was abundant evidence on which the jury could find as they did'.

Dennis Howard was executed at Winson Green on 4 December, the first person to be hanged there under the new Homicide Act, and also the first hanging without a crowd of people present. (There had been one other hanging since the reintroduction of the death penalty earlier that year – that of twenty-one-year-old William Vickers, who had murdered a seventy-two-year-old shopkeeper in Carlisle.)

'It was a sad end for an unfortunate young man who happened to have an unhealthy interest in guns,' Mr Fishwick told me.

The one man to come out of the case with official credit was Detective Superintendent George Miller. At the end of the trial Mr Justice Hinchcliffe drew attention to '... what I regard as the brave conduct of Detective Superintendent Miller for grabbing Howard on the stairs of his home when he could have held a loaded gun. His conduct was in keeping with the highest traditions of the police and deserving of the highest praise.'

Footnote: The Dudley Herald newspaper reported that David Keasey had been filling in the time between customers reading a book. Its title? *One, Two, Buckle My Shoe*, a story dealing with the shooting of a dentist, the crime solved, of course, by Agatha Christie's famous detective Hercule Poirot.

6   Wife-Killer, Willenhall, 1872

Stafford Assizes: Mr Motteram, counsel for the defence, summing up, said that in order to find the prisoner guilty of murder, it was necessary that the jury should be satisfied that what he had done had been done maliciously – with malice aforethought.

That was the crux; for this is no 'whodunit'. Everyone knew that Christopher Edwards had killed his wife Rosannah with a poker at around ten o'clock on the night of 30 April 1872.

The case had all the ingredients of a Victorian melodrama: screams of murder, a shadowy figure seen from across the street against the candlelight of an upstairs room, a weapon raised in the hand, and lots of blood – an estimated 1½ pints on the bedroom floor.

Christopher and Rosannah Edwards, both aged thirty-four, lived with their two surviving children in Church Street, Willenhall, in a typical two-up, two-down terrace house, one of the many thousands built to cope with the huge increase in population as people poured into Black Country towns during the Industrial Revolution of the late eighteenth and early nineteenth centuries. Such houses were built so that the staircase upper landing separated the two bedrooms, a fact of some significance to the story.

The house in which the Edwards family lived was close to the junction of Church Street with Froysell Street, next to a school connected with Froysell Chapel and close to Doctor's Piece, used as a burial ground for 211 cholera victims in the 1849 epidemic. In 1988 there is not a private dwelling left in either, just an unsightly conglomeration of industrial premises, with a section of Church Street blocked off. The chapel is disused and in a derelict state, but happily Doctor's Piece remains a well-kept area of green protected by iron railings.

Christopher Edwards was a locksmith – hardly surprising since Willenhall was (and still is) Britain's main centre of lockmaking, traditionally earning the town the nickname 'Umpshire', by reason of the humpbacks of the lock-filers' stooping all day over their benches. The main lockmaking firms are today strongly entrenched: Josiah Parkes, who market their locks under the trade name 'Union', after the street of that name which originally housed their Willenhall premises, and Yale Security Products – Yale being the name of the founder.

This then is the heritage that people like Edwards helped to create, although he was actually employed by one of the many smaller firms, Alexander Lloyd & Sons of Stafford Street, where he worked for fourteen years. As was the practice, he in turn employed an apprentice who referred to him as 'master' and lodged with the family. The Edwards occupied one bedroom and he slept in the other, just across the landing. His name was George Marsh, and he was aged sixteen at the time.

During the early part of Tuesday 30 April Edwards was at work, but when a class of work with which he was unfamiliar was placed before him, he left in a bad temper and visited a public house, arriving home the worse for drink. It was well-known that he drank – though most men 'went boozing' in those slave-driving times – but it was also known that his worst fault was jealousy, particularly as regards his wife. He had developed a fixation that she was 'after someone', and this had developed into a mania. Neighbours said that Rosannah could not look at a man without angering her husband. There was absolutely no reason.

Rosannah, the daughter of a bricklayer at Bloxwich, had

married Edwards twelve years before, and they had had four children, those still living, being Regina, aged five, and Laura, who was four. They had lived in Church Street for three years.

James Adey, Edwards' next-door neighbour, called on Edwards at about nine o'clock that evening. It seemed to him that Edwards was sober and that he and his wife were on good terms. He left after about three-quarters of an hour. Shortly afterwards he heard Rosannah screaming and ran outdoors and tried to get into the house, but both doors were fastened. He immediately raised the chill cry of 'Murder! ... Police!' and people poured from their houses, but although they could see the shadow of a man beating at something in the bedroom, they did not attempt to force an entrance. (One has to look at their reluctance to interfere from the standpoint of the day, when it was usual, even commonplace, for a Black Country man to beat his wife – within reason, of course.)

Three policemen arrived: Inspector Gasson and Constables Anderton and Bakewell, having heard that there was 'dreadful work' going on in Church Street. They tried the front door, then went round the back and attempted to get in by the back door. Under the circumstances, they appeared very leisurely about it, and by the time they returned to the street, the neighbours, emboldened by the presence of the law, had broken down the front door. They found Edwards seated on the bottom step of the stairs covered in blood. In one hand he held a candlestick with a lighted candle; in the other he cradled his daughter Laura.

As PC Bakewell grabbed him, Edwards asked what they all wanted. Then he added, 'I'm the man.' Upstairs they found the body of Rosannah lying face down on the bed in such a position that her knees almost touched her chin. There was much blood, and she had a large wound behind the right ear. She was dressed, even to her shoes, and there were signs of a struggle.

Both the children must have witnessed the tragedy.

Edwards was promptly charged with the murder of his wife. On the way to the police station he said, 'Tell old Lloyd [his employer] I shan't be making any more lock-pins for him.'

The inquest opened at the Artillery Inn, Lower Lichfield Street, Willenhall, on 2 May, before the deputy coroner. It was learned that the deceased had been of irreproachable character, clean in her habits and attentive to housework. Neighbours declared that Edwards had wronged his wife by his jealousy. When her husband had been in one of his rages, usually after drinking on Saturday nights, it was not unusual for her to seek refuge in one of their houses, staying all night. Also, the girl Regina was intelligent and could tell when her mother was about to be attacked. She too would escape to another house 'while he was going to give mother a thrashing'.

Again, no one had sought to interfere.

It came to light that Rosannah was convinced that Edwards would kill her, and she had said so to friends. On the Monday week before she was killed she had taken a carving-knife and an axe to a neighbour, afraid, she said, that her husband would use them upon her.

On the Tuesday following, Rosannah had told neighbours that it was 'a good job I left the chopper and knife'. She explained that her husband had got up three times in the night, and although she had asked him what he wanted, he could not say.

Seemingly, she was suspicious of his every move. Friends and relatives alike feared for her, and she had often been invited to go and live with her brother at nearby Moxley. Fear prevented her. She declared that Edwards had threatened to shoot her if she left him.

Edwards was committed for trial at the next Stafford Assizes and shortly afterwards was said to have spoken of Rosannah as an excellent wife, denying that his crime resulted from jealousy. 'She was bad-tempered,' he said, a statement rather at odds with her being 'excellent'. 'Drink was the cause of it all.'

The funeral took place on a Sunday, and over 100,000 people were estimated to have witnessed the event, morbid curiosity ever strong. A collection made among the crowd for Edwards' two children produced £2 14s.6d., whilst in other parts of the town £15 was raised – a respectable sum in those days.

That same evening the Reverend G. H. Fisher preached at the parish church of St Giles from the text '... whoso sheddeth a man's blood, by man shall his blood be shed, for in the image of God made He man' (Genesis, 9:6). Alluding to the murder, Fisher said that he had read in a Birmingham newspaper that within the last ten years the annals of Willenhall had been stained by the record of four murders.

'Although unhappily true,' he went on, 'it ought to be made known that, of the four, only Christopher Edwards belonged to the parish by birth and parentage: his ancestors might be traced back in the parish for several generations. Not only that, his crime was more atrocious than any of the previous three. Edwards had been a scholar in St Giles schools. He was a sullen, morose, vengeful lad, the taunt of playmates, among who he made few, if any, friends.'

So the good Reverend went on, berating Edwards' character in a way that would not be entertained today before a trial. However, if he sought to whitewash Willenhall, he failed, for it was well known as a violent place, as evidenced by the Children's Employment Commission Report of thirty years earlier – a report said to have been drawn upon by Disraeli for his novel *Sybil*. Change was slow. In fact, on the very day of Edwards' execution, we read of a fifty-year-old shoemaker being kicked to death by three or four men. Yes: another murder!

During the long wait for the summer assizes, a matter of some twelve weeks, interest would have waned and, indeed many men, if they thought of it at all, would have considered Edwards to be unfortunate in having, as they used to put it, 'struck an unlucky blow'. Indeed, Willenhall experienced almost a copy-cat murder when the same PC Anderton who had gone to Edwards' house was called to the home of one John Taylor Davis by the latter's sister-in-law, who said that Davis was killing his wife. Anderton found Davis with a poker in his hand.

Mrs Davis had been lucky that time, but the magistrate declared: 'These things are becoming so common, we shall have to put a stop to them. We are going back into a state of barbarianism.'

The trial of Christopher Edwards opened on 27 July before Mr Justice Quain (1816-76, knighted 1872), with Mr Boughey for the prosecution and, by the request of his lordship, Mr Motteram defending.

Boughey detailed the facts of Rosannah's character as a clean, hardworking woman, and that of her husband as being harsh and unkind, yet consumed with jealousy. 'There were no grounds for any jealous feeling on the part of the prisoner towards his wife,' he told the jury. 'Even if there had been, it did not justify them in reducing the crime from murder to manslaughter.'

As evidence of the deceased's anticipation of further ill-usage, he related how she had taken the knife and chopper to a neighbour eight days before her murder. 'Of course, he could only give the jury this fact and it would be for them to draw the inference. In fairness to the prisoner he ought to mention to them that she *might* have taken the articles with an innocent intention, without any fear that they might be made use of against her by the prisoner. Bearing in mind that upon the following Sunday she fetched back the carving-knife (to cut the Sunday joint) it was clear that she had no apprehension with respect to that particular weapon.'

But everyone knew that Rosannah was scared out of her wits. It had been in all the papers.

The first witness was George Marsh, Edwards' apprentice, who lived in his master's house. Mrs Edwards was, he declared, a good woman who had treated him well – a decided plus, for many apprentices were dreadfully abused. He told the court that he had come home at about nine o'clock and found Mrs Edwards in the front room, in her usual spirits. He sat in the back kitchen for about twenty minutes and then went to bed. Yes: he knew that a poker was kept in the kitchen, but could not say if it was there that evening.

When Marsh retired, Edwards and his wife were in the front room. He had been in bed for some thirty minutes when he heard Mrs Edwards scream, 'George … George … George!' He had not been to sleep, had heard no quarrelling or shouting and heard no more until Edwards came into his room. He had a poker in one hand and a candlestick with a lighted candle in the other.

'He asked me if I was all right. I said yes, and he said, "That's all right, me lad," and left the room. Then he returned and said, "George, me lad, you are out of your time [meaning his apprenticeship was at an end.] You just get up and take the children to your father, and your sister will come from Moxley and look after them."

'He also said to me, Marsh went on, "I have not done this over you" ' – obviously anxious to remove any doubt that he thought his apprentice had been 'carrying on' with his wife. ' "I love you too well to do anything to you. Tell Mr Lloyd I am not going to work for him any more. I am going to die on the scaffold." Then he kissed me and left the room.'

Marsh went on to say that he had dressed, gone downstairs and found Edwards with the children. 'The first time he came into my room I noticed blood on his hands and shirt and apron. I said, "I hope you binna gonna do anything to me,'' because I was frightened.' He said he had lived at the house for two years, during which time the prisoner had treated his wife badly. He had turned her out on Saturday nights when he had been drinking, and not let her back in. The last time he had done so was a fortnight before her death. It had, so far as Marsh knew, been a long time since Edwards had actually struck her, although he ran after her intending to do so whenever he turned her out.

Cross-examined by Mr Motteram, Marsh said that Edwards had been good to him, except when he was in drink. No: he had never seen Mrs Edwards sharp with her husband or pick a quarrel.

'I left home about seven o'clock on the night Mrs Edwards was killed. Edwards passed me in the entry, coming in as I went out.'

Re-examined, Marsh said Edwards had clearly been drinking.

So ended the questioning of this youth whose evidence was so vital, yet so odd in one important detail. He was in bed across the landing and, asleep or awake, how could he have failed to hear the commotion when it was clearly heard next door? He admitted having heard Rosannah cry out his name three times. Why had he not gone to her assistance, since surely he recognized it as a plea for help? Likely enough he had heard the blows struck and was frightened for his own life.

No one pressed him on his possible perjury.

James Adey was called. He too was a locksmith and lived next door to the Edwards. He told how earlier on the night of the murder he had been in Edwards' house and had seen the prisoner and his wife, who was nursing the younger child. They had discussed horse-racing. As for the screams he had heard from his own house (only one thickness of brick separated dwellings of this type), he had '... never heard anything the like'.

He said he was the first person to reach the street. He

shouted for help, and people came running from all directions. 'I then went back into my own house and put my boots on,' he told the court, careful not to miss a detail.

Under cross-examination Adey said that Mrs Edwards was a quiet woman. He had known her for three years and had never seen her in a rage. In answer to a question from the judge, he said he had not heard the prisoner's voice through the wall. 'Only when the police took him.'

Adey's wife, Sarah, followed. At a quarter-past-seven on 30 April she had seen Rosannah in her yard. She remembered her husband coming from Edwards' house and, after they had gone to bed, hearing a scream. 'I knew it was Rosannah. I had often heard her scream when she had run out of her house. She had several times spent a night in our house for fear of her husband. I followed my husband into the street. I saw a light in Edwards' front room and saw it carried into the back room.'

She revealed that on the day before the crime she had met Rosannah in the town. 'She asked me if her husband had come back home. I told her that he had and she said "I must hurry to him." She had been in the town on an errand and I afterwards heard him say to her several times that she had been to see someone, and that "she should not go many times more, for he would do for her." '

Under cross-examination, Mrs Adey said she did not hear quarrelling prior to the scream, adding, 'Rosannah told me on Tuesday morning that she did not know what she would do, as her husband had been on at her threatening the same as the day before. She never provoked him that I know of. When he ill-used her, she ran away.'

Re-examined, Sarah Adey said, 'I do not remember her ever using bad language towards him. I thought he used to get on to her because he was jealous, but knew of no reason for it.'

Next to take the stand was Sylvanus Dare, a locksmith of Willenhall, who stated that, at about a few minutes to ten on the night in question, he heard a disturbance in the street and went to Edwards' house. 'I put my ear to the keyhole of the door. I heard a scream, then a moan in the house. Looking up to the front-room window, I saw a light disappear from there and show in the downstairs room. It returned in about a minute. When I first saw the light, I heard three blows upstairs and then something being broken.'

There is surely a discrepancy here, for Adey said he was the first person to reach the street, so that by the time Dare put his ear to the keyhole the fateful blows should have been struck. However, his story was not challenged, and he went on to tell of the arrival of the police and of the door being broken down. He then saw the prisoner '... with lots of blood on his hands and apron. Before anything was said to him, Edwards said, "I have done it. Will you let me lace my boots before you take me?" '

Dare told Mr Motteram that he had known Edwards for three years and had never known him quarrelsome except when drunk.

A blacksmith named John Pettie was then called. He had been near the house of the prisoner, whom he had known for seven years, when he heard that something was the matter there. 'I stood over the road. There was a candle in the upstairs front room. Edwards held it. I saw him leave the room, and two minutes later he came back and stood the light on the mantelpiece. I saw him strike three or four blows near the fireplace. I could see he had something in his hand: like a poker. I ran 150 yards to the police station and returned with the constables. While the door was being broken down, I saw Edwards in a stooping position, as if trying to pick up something and put it on the bed.'

This last bit of evidence was immediately corroborated by the next witness, Henry Quantrell.

But, somehow, doesn't the timing seem all wrong? It can only be accounted for if the scream was heard several minutes before the blows were struck, and in a volatile society it is odd that it merited such prompt response, except, of course, by the apprentice Marsh, who, had *he* responded, could possibly have prevented the tragedy.

PC Bakewell gave evidence of the scene in the house, the body and the gore, and the arrest of Edwards, who had said, after being charged, 'She started it. I finished it. I don't think she is dead. She hadn't ought to be. I don't think they will give me more than twelve months. I didn't do it wilfully. She has been a good wife to me.'

So he did not think she was dead. Yet he had already told Marsh that he would go to the gallows.'

Confirming his colleague's statement, PC Anderston added that, whilst Edwards was in the passage at the police station, he had said, 'She was very cross-tempered, and so am I. I shall meet her in Heaven. You'll find me at Stafford [assizes] to be as I am now.'

The Willenhall police inspector, Walter Gasson, then told the court how he had found the dead body of Rosannah Edwards, and also the poker, which he exhibited. It was in the fender of the downstairs room and had fresh blood upon it; also a long hair at the top. Edwards had told him, 'Sorry! It's a pity.'

Next came the surgeon, John Thomas Harthill, who said he had examined the body. It was lying face downward on the bed in a small pool of blood. 'A cut two inches long extended to the bone on the right eyebrow. There was an extensive fracture at the base of the skull behind the right ear. A large quantity of blood was on the floor, and blood was spattered on the fireplace and walls.

'At the post-mortem examination I removed twenty-seven pieces of bone, and these did not include the whole of the fracture. Bone had not penetrated the brain, but the brain was compressed. The poker could have caused such an injury. Great violence had been used, and the cause of death was fracture of the skull. I took from the poker a long hair, similar to that of the deceased.'

Questioned by the judge, he gave it as his opinion that the body had been placed on the bed after the injuries had been inflicted.

The case for the prosecution now at an end, Mr Motteram addressed the jury on behalf of the prisoner. 'It was,' he said, 'idle for him, after what had been heard, to deny that it was the prisoner that had caused the woman's death, for the evidence had established the fact. But although the woman had died at the hand of the prisoner, it did not follow as a necessary legal consequence that he had been guilty of the awful crime of murder.'

He went on to tell the jury that they must be satisfied that the prisoner's act had been malicious. If they found an absence of malice, which the law required to be established for the crime of murder, the homicide must be reduced from murder to manslaughter. He then outlined the facts which he believed might help the jury in reaching their verdict, and expressed a wish that witnesses had been called to enable the character of the prisoner to be ascertained.

True enough; neither Edwards' employer nor his workmates had been called, only neighbours who could possibly be biased.

'The jury being men of the world,' Motteram continued, subjecting them to a nice flattering touch (no women, mark you), 'were not to suppose that every woman was an angel and every man a monster.' Developing this theme, he brought out points he believed favourable to his client, harping on the fact that on the day before the murder the deceased had gone into Willenhall town '... evidently without her husband's knowledge and certainly without his consent, and had hastened back guiltily when she learned he was at home'.

Such were the accepted standards of the time, and Motteram was trying hard to show that Rosannah was not above deceiving her husband. He ended by asking the jury to consider that the prisoner's act was the result of some sudden quarrel, giving rise to an uncontrollable fit of passion, and that sufficient provocation had been given to justify the reduction of the crime to one of manslaughter.

Summing up, Mr Justice Quain told the jury that they had to consider whether the crime was one of manslaughter or of murder. He must direct that, '… prima facie, if a man took away the life of another, the law presumed that he did it as an act of malice aforethought, unless evidence was shown to the contrary. If the crime was exasperated by any sudden quarrel, it must be shown that provocation was given to justify his using a poker before the crime could be reduced to manslaughter.'

It took the jury only a few minutes to return a verdict of guilty.

Black cap on head, the judge told Edwards that he had scarcely ever heard of a worse case of wife-murder. 'You have habitually ill-treated this wretched woman for a series of years, and I am afraid she must have spent a most wretched life in trying to live in the same house with you.'

He then pronounced sentence of death.

That the case against Edwards was even worse than the judge had pictured became evident in the contents of a letter which the former dictated in prison whilst awaiting execution. He related how he had left work early and, '… on my way home, as I passed the Shakespeare Inn, I was called by William Cooper, Josiah Tonks and Charles Bateman. I remained drinking with them and others until half past seven. When I went home, I was the worse for drink. James Adey came in, and after he had gone, we had supper and I read the paper for a short time. It was then I resolved to kill my wife that night and, fearing that if I took the poker upstairs she might take alarm, I left my snuff-box on the table as an excuse for going down again.'

Edwards told how, when he returned for his snuff-box, he took the poker and returned to the bedroom. 'My wife was near the doorway, and turned towards it. I struck her on the forehead with the poker. She cried "George" three times, I think, and I gave her another blow on the top of the head, which caused her to fall across the bed. She did not move or make any cry. I jumped over the bed, between my wife and the head of the bed, and, placing the poker by the fireplace, seized her by the throat with both hands and strangled her.'

Strangled her! Here was a sensation. All the detail of a trial and no mention of strangulation. Why had not the surgeon spotted this important fact?

Edwards' revelations went on. 'My right hand and arms, being under her chin and resting on my knees, were covered with blood from the wounds, so also was my right leg. Having held her in this position for some minutes, I let go and her head dropped over the side of the bed, where a pool of blood formed.'

So the surgeon was wrong again: the body had not been on the floor and then lifted onto the bed, as he had surmised in court.

There was more. 'Grasping the poker once more,' the confession went on, 'I dealt her several blows about the back of the head, and at this time I think I must have been in my violence, for I knocked over the candle which was on the chimney-piece. I went downstairs for a light, and on my return to the bedroom I placed the body of my wife lengthways on the bed, as it was found. Taking the poker, the candle and my younger child (I have no recollection of even seeing the elder at that moment), I went to George Marsh's room as he stated.'

Declaring this to be a true account, Edwards added: 'There was no quarrel, nor had there been any words between my wife and myself since the previous Saturday evening, but often, under the influence of drink which always inflamed my jealous feeling, I had resolved to murder her. My wife was a good, hardworking woman, and if I had been ruled by her, we should have been the happiest couple in the land … Drink has been my ruin, and is the ruin of most of the men of my class of life in that neighbourhood. May they all take warning from my unhappy fate.'

The Temperance Movement would have been highly delighted with that. By coincidence, a few days before the execution, upward of 200 Black Country children held a summer treat organized by various abstinence bodies, such as the Band of Hope.

On the Monday before the execution Edwards was visited by several relatives, including his younger daughter, Laura. The elder child was not brought to the prison because she had witnessed the tragedy and it was thought that she should not see her father again.

One wonders how much she remembered of that bloody assault in the bedroom, and to what extent it coloured her adult life.

Christopher Edwards was executed at Stafford on 13 August. His was the first hanging to take place in private at this particular gaol. Immediately the drop fell and the body was seen hanging perfectly still, it was remarked by an official, 'How easy he has gone.' However, after a few seconds there was movement, and for at least two minutes '... his struggles were painfully evident', so much so that a witness was driven to comment that he had never known one to die harder.

Postscript: The body was lain in a little burial ground behind the prison chapel, near the remains of a murderer named Collier who had been executed in August 1866.

The executioner of both men was Smith, 'The Dudley Hangman', as he was widely known. As we have seen, he made a poor job of despatching Edwards, but he had made a real botch of it when he hanged Collier six years earlier.

Collier was a North Staffordshire man, and his crime has no place in this book, but hangman Smith certainly has, for he lived in a cottage in the district of Oakham, one of the highest points in the Black Country – there is still a public house called 'The Hangman's Tree' to remind one of a gruesome, if happily rare occupation. He was nominally an agricultural labourer.

William Collier was the last person to be hanged in public at Stafford Gaol. Smith joined two pieces of rope insecurely, so that, when the floor fell, Collier disappeared from view, instead of hanging by the neck. There was a great commotion, and people in the crowd cried, 'It's a miracle!' thinking that Collier would now surely be reprieved.

Not at all. The prison governor had other ideas. Another rope was brought, and the thoroughly unnerved Smith actually apologized to Collier before successfully hanging him at his second attempt.

Christopher Edwards was his last 'victim', for he died in the following year. However, there are still many tales circulating in Dudley about their own nineteenth century hangman.

7 Wage-Snatch Leads to Murder, Dudley, 1878

The Black Country of 1878 was coming to the end of a three-year trade slump that was among the worst of the nineteenth-century depressions. The western part of the borough of Dudley was a conglomeration of pits and ironworks, many of the former exhausted and derelict, with new ones opened up close by. It was criss-crossed by dirt tracks and lanes, and had in parts something of a moonscape appearance, yet for all that still retained enough industrial activity to retain the famous 'Black by day and red by night' image bestowed upon it a decade earlier by an American consul based in Birmingham.

Thus any part of the district described as 'lonely' has to be assessed against this background, for, as our murderer was to find to his cost, all was not quite as it seemed when he attacked his chosen victim.

The firm of Hill & Smith, Brierley Hill, Dudley, was founded in 1824 and still exists today on its original site at the end of Canal Street, a cul-de-sac or 'pudding-bag street'. An ironworks of great repute (had it not in 1860 received a testimonial from Balmoral for supplying 'many miles' of fencing to Queen Victoria?), it was in fair shape when, early on the afternoon of Friday 6 December 1878, their clerk Alfred Meredith, set off for Dudley, two miles distant, to collect the weekly wages from the bank. Since he lived near the town and walked the distance daily, he had long since worked out the shortest route and did not take the main road which we know today as the A461 bu headed off through the district of Woodside towards Parkhead, where the famous canal 'legging tunnel' emerges after passing beneath the town from Tipton, and made a beeline for the soaring spire of St Thomas' Church, a landmark for miles around.

Meredith collected from the bank a black bag containing £280 6s. 9d. and set off on his return journey to the works. At an early stage he realized that he was being followed, a fact which he admitted later in hospital when he stated, 'I did not look back or it might have been thought that I was afraid.'

He had cause to be: that was the only statement he was able to make.

The area Meredith had to traverse was littered with old pit mounds and workings, with the occasional pit still operating, and doubtless Meredith's pursuer felt fairly safe when, somewhere between Parkhead and Woodside, he came up with him and shot the young clerk in the face and neck with a pistol, rapidly making off with the money.

However, if he thought there was no one around, he was very much mistaken. Help for Meredith was quickly forthcoming. Later several witnesses would say that they had seen the assailant immediately before or had heard the shot. A crowd gathered and Meredith was taken to the Guest Hospital on the far side of Dudley, opened only nine years previously.

The bag was found some 200 yards from the spot, still containing £5 in silver – indicative of the thief's haste – plus a letter from the bank to Hill & Smith. The police were summoned, and Chief Superintendent Burton and other officers arrived, preliminary enquiries rapidly leading them to suspect a twenty-year-old, slim-built fellow named Enoch Whiston, who had been employed as a horse-driver and labourer. He lived between Hill & Smith's works and Woodside and may well have spotted Meredith on earlier journeys to the bank and marked him down.

Further enquiries led the police to a house in Commonside, Pensnett, occupied by a twenty-three-year-old woman named Mary Terry, with whom Whiston 'kept company', as the saying then was. And, indeed, there he was found in hiding. A search revealed £9 in silver, found in a coat, together with a pistol, at which stage Whiston was apprehended. The woman had £25 in gold in her purse. Both were taken to Brierley Hill Police Station, where it was discovered that the pistol was loaded with 'rough slugs of brass'.

No doubt realizing the hopelessness of his position, Whiston did not deny the crime, telling the police that he had thrown the rest of the money away.

On the following day, at Dudley Police Station, Whiston was charged with robbery and the attempted murder of Alfred Meredith, and Terry with having received money knowing it to have been stolen. They were remanded until the following Wednesday.

Meanwhile details of Meredith's injuries began to filter through to the waiting crowd. He had received the full force of the discharge from the pistol and had a wound immediately behind the right ear and a skull fracture. He was unconscious, and there seemed little hope.

At about 3.30 on the Saturday morning, Whiston asked to make a statement, in which he admitted having trailed Meredith and that when he had arrived at a lonely part of the road he had fired at only a few paces distant. Seeing the result of his shot, he ran through a hedge and hid in a hollow between two cinder mounds, extracted all the money, as he thought, from the bag and threw it away.

When he came to the Fens Pool (a canal feeder reservoir, and scene of many accidental drownings), Whiston secreted the bulk of the money in the vicinity of the pool and subsequently divided the rest with Terry. He declared that he had not seen any paper money, and no more gold than that accounted for. 'The bag fell open as I ran away. I suppose the rest fell out.'

Superintendent Burton promptly had Whiston conveyed to the Fens Pool, and the prisoner pointed out a
hiding-place which contained £40 in silver. However, this
prospect of money being scattered all over the area caused
a miniature gold-rush among the local inhabitants, and it
was reported that hundreds of persons searched the
byways, but nothing came to the knowledge of the police.
The motives of these searchers may have been mixed but,
as events were to show, any self-interested searcher could
not have appropriated more than a couple of pounds.

The police pressed Whiston to disclose where he had
hidden the rest of the money, not believing his story, and
on the Monday he was again taken to the Fens Pool,
where he obligingly pointed to a spot. As he well knew,
nothing would be found there.

Meredith regained consciousness on the Tuesday
morning and asked to see Burton, and it was then that he
just managed to whisper that he had known he was being
followed, before again becoming unfit for questioning.

Wednesday found the prisoners before the bench to
hear the charge once more. Mary Terry was weeping, but
Enoch Whiston had entered the dock with ' ... a
swaggering gait ... not seeming to appreciate his position'.
Tall and slim, with a boyish look, he was respectably
dressed but appeared to show little interest in the
proceedings.

Mary Terry was dealt with first, it being said on her
behalf that she had had nothing to do with the crime and
knew nothing further of the money. She had planned to
be engaged to Whiston on the day before Christmas and
was expecting a sum of money from him, which he told
her he had saved, keeping it in a hole in the wall of the
pantry at his mother's house. Immediately the police had
arrived at her house she had surrendered the £25 Whiston
had given her. Her story was accepted and she was
discharged.

Chief Superintendent Burton then asked for a remand

for Whiston for one week on the charge of highway robbery wth violence (not yet murder). He told the court that he had that morning received from the hospital surgeon a statement that he believed would justify his asking for a remand without tendering evidence.

The magistrate's clerk then read out a letter which said that Meredith was much worse and in a critical condition. 'I fear he cannot live,' the letter ended, whereupon Whiston's legal representative said that he would not object to a remand. He expressed sympathy for the injured man on behalf of Whiston's parents and friends. The remand was granted.

Alfred Meredith died on the following afternoon, and Whiston was informed and charged with wilful murder, responding with a look of 'the wildest terror', as well he might. He was taken to his cell and almost immediately shouted, 'Oh, Mr Burton, I wish you would bring me out before the fire. Since you told me that, I feel so awful cold.'

Surprisingly, perhaps, his wish was complied with, and as he sat down, Whiston burst into tears and asked if it was true that Meredith was dead. Burton told him gently that it was. He was clearly a kind officer and indeed was greatly respected, serving for thirty-six years before his retirement in 1893.

The inquest took place on 13 December, when the coroner, Mr Robert Watts, opened an inquiry at the Guest Hospital. A legal representative was sent to watch over the proceedings on behalf of Whiston, and Mr Henry Hill, of the firm of Hill & Smith, was also present. The jury viewed the body, and after Thomas Meredith had confirmed that it was that of his brother Alfred, Annie Waite, a nurse, testified that Meredith had died on the Thursday afternoon in the presence of one of his friends. Having ascertained from Burton that he had a man in custody for the murder, and learning that Whiston was to appear before the magistrates on the following Wednesday, the coroner adjourned the inquiry until four o'clock that same

Wednesday. Since the witnesses would all be at the town hall, he said, it would be convenient for the inquest to resume there. Meantime, a post-mortem would be made.

That same afternoon Whiston again saw Burton and declared that he would point out where he had hidden the bag containing the missing gold. He was then taken to Commonside and, after traversing several pit mounds, led the police to a ditch and pulled from a hole a bag containing £200 in notes and gold, and 5s. 9d. in small change. Handing it over, he smiled and said, 'I don't think anybody in the world could have found it.'

Less than £2 of the stolen money remained unrecovered.

At the resumed hearing, large crowds gathered outside the town hall, only a small number being able to gain admittance. The proceedings began with Mr J. L. Holberton prosecuting for Hill & Smith, and Mr Harper, of Messrs Stokes & Harper, defending. Holberton said there was little doubt that the prisoner was the man accused of the death of Alfred Meredith, and as the deceased had occupied a position of trust in the firm for some years, they felt 'deeply interested in his terrible fate'. It would be proved conclusively that the prisoner had watched the deceased leave the bank. He explained that Meredith did not take the usual route but instead one more direct for himself, '… unfortunately, that in which the prisoner was better able to commit the deed'. Praising Chief Superintendent Burton and his colleagues, he declared, 'Never had a murderer met with a more prompt apprehension.'

As we shall see, no inspired detective work was needed, for, as witnesses were called, Whiston could have wished he had chosen a different spot for his crime.

Henry Griffin Walker, manager of the Birmingham, Dudley & District Banking Company, said that he remembered Meredith's coming to the bank on the afternoon of 6 December. 'It was usual to come for the cash on that day,' he said, and he listed in detail the composition of the money placed in the bag. He had entered the numbers of the notes on the back of Hill & Smith's cheque.

Mary Lilly was then called. She told how she had met Meredith, whom she described as 'a little man with a black bag', on that fateful afternoon. Moreover, she had seen him on previous occasions on Fridays at around the same time. On each occasion the time was between two and three o'clock in the afternoon, and he had been heading in the direction of Hill & Smith.

Daniel Round then gave evidence that on that afternoon he had seen both the prisoner and the deceased, Meredith going first and Whiston following, about three paces away. Both had passed him, and after he had walked about a hundred yards, he heard the report of a firearm. He returned to the scene and saw a pool of blood and someone already helping the deceased to a house. He did not see who had fired the shot.

Harriet Bradford, a widow living at Woodside, almost opposite what was then Pit Lane, leading to Hill & Smith, was one of those who had helped Meredith. She said she had heard what sounded like a pistol shot and had run to where she could see a man struggling. 'It was the same man who had the bag. Directly afterwards I saw the prisoner run up the field towards the pool with a bag in his hand, similar to that the other man had. I helped the injured man up and, assisted by a man named Wall, got him to a nearby public house. There I washed his face. He was bleeding behind the right ear and would not let me wash there.'

Isaac Wall spoke next. A licensed victualler at the British Lion, Woodside, he was in the vicinity that afternoon when he too heard the shot and found Meredith struggling on the ground. He also saw the prisoner run off, and his evidence that '… he had previously known the prisoner Whiston and his father' could have been the key statement in enabling Whiston's arrest in a remarkably short time. Wall confirmed that he had helped Harriet Bradford get Meredith to a public house, known as Jubbs.

James Buckley, an engineer on duty that day at an engine-house in Pit Lane, was told by a banksman (pit bank worker) that a man had been shot. When he reached the spot, Meredith had been removed, but he looked at the pool of blood and '… saw something like iron in it. I found it was a leaden slug and gave it to Mr Stevens, a clerk at Hill & Smiths.'

Thomas Smith, a miner at Woodside Colliery, next gave evidence. He was at work when he heard a pistol shot and looked to see Meredith lying on the ground. 'I went to the spot and when I saw a man run off I went after him. Up the first field I found the bag under a hedge. There was a packet containing money and a letter. I came back and gave it to one of Hill & Smith's clerks.'

The clerk referred to was Thomas Sanders Stevens, a colleague of Meredith at the firm. 'Every Friday afternoon it was customary for him [Meredith] to go to the bank for money to pay the wages, and he used to take the black leather bag now produced.' Stevens had known the prisoner for some years, because up to 'recent time' Whiston had been in the employ of Hill & Smith. When news of the shooting reached the firm, Stevens had reported to his boss and hurried to the scene, where he was handed the money-bag by the witness, Thomas Smith. After checking the contents, he gave it to PC Staines.

This officer told the court that he was stationed at Woodside, only about eighty yards from the incident. 'I was at home and heard the report of a firearm.' His timing was precise – 3.30. 'I went outside but did not see anything. Soon afterwards I heard something from a passer-by and ran across the fields to Pit Lane.' He described what he had found and how he had asked Meredith who had done it. 'The deceased attempted to speak, but his mouth was full of blood. I advised that the injured man be taken to Jubb's public house, and went in pursuit of the assailant.

'After ten minutes I gave up, having seen nothing of the prisoner, and returned to the scene of the crime, where I took possession from Mr Stevens of the black bag, a packet of silver, and a leaden slug covered with blood. That same night I went to Brierley Hill Police Station and saw the prisoner in custody. He was given into my charge and in the course of a few minutes said, "Are they going to lock the girl up?" I said "Very likely," and then he asked if they had taken all the money off her. I told him that they had and he went on to make the following statement: "I lost some of it as I was coming across the field. I put in my hand to take out some money, and the bag fell open, and some was upset on the ground. After I shot him I was so frightened. I was afraid I had killed him. I did not intend to kill him.'

Cross-examined, PC Staines said there were no houses in Pit Lane, and the engine-house was the nearest building but completely hidden by a large pit mound. Crossing the fields pointed out by witnesses would lead in a direct line to the Fens Pool, and Commonside, where Mary Terry lived, was further on in the same direction.

In answer to a question from Mr Harper, PC Staines said that Mary Terry had been sitting in another room when the conversation with Whiston took place at the police station. 'She could see us, as the door was opened, but could not hear what was said. When the prisoner began to make his statement, I did not caution him and say it would be used in evidence against him.'

Mary Terry took the stand, describing herself as a single woman. She had known Whiston for about six months. 'I saw him on 5 December. We were on the point of being married, and it was to have taken place the day before Christmas Day. About a month before he told me he had been saving money and had about £30. He said he would give me £25 and keep £5 for himself.' Whiston had told her he was going to get a job in Shropshire, and on the Friday of the crime he had come to her house at about half past four.

'He often complained of the headache, and I thought that day he was not right. He gave me a purse of money, asking me to take care of it, and when he did so he said, "Oh, my head is bad." As I took the money upstairs, I heard a knock at the door and when I came down I saw that PC Keenan had hold of the prisoner, and he was charged with shooting and robbing Meredith. I said, "Oh Lord, come with me quick," and an officer went upstairs with me and I gave him the purse of money."

Next called was PC John Keenan, who had gone to Terry's house with two other officers. Apparently he knew her well, for he called her Polly. He described how, when the prisoner opened the door to him, '... he sprang into the corner of the kitchen where his jacket was lying on the back of a chair.' Keenan told how he had seized the jacket and found a pistol in the right-hand pocket. 'It was loaded to the muzzle, and with the charge on the table. The pistol was capped and contained two slugs similar to that found near where the deceased was shot, except that they were not flattened as much.'

Chief Superintendent Burton then told how he had received the prisoner at Dudley, and how Whiston had led him a dance, taking him on fruitless searches for the money until at last he had 'come clean' and led him to Commonside, where the bulk of the money was found. On that occasion, during the return journey, Whiston had said, 'Mr Burton, you have made a mistake in calling it a slug. They were not slugs in the pistol, they were bullets. I flattened them between two bricks to make them fit tighter.'

Frank Goulder, a resident surgeon at Dudley Guest Hospital, was called next. He said Meredith had been partially conscious when brought in. Having attended him until his death, he had carried out the post-mortem in company with a senior surgeon. 'I found an abscess on the brain containing three pieces of lead or slugs [produced] and three small pieces of bone. The cause of death was the abscess ... I have no doubt at all that death was caused by shooting.'

Thus far the evidence given had centred on the scene of the crime and the swift action of the police in making an arrest, along with the subsequent toing-and-froing with the prisoner in search of the missing money. But important evidence now came from another quarter, when a Mrs Sarah Humphrey was called. She explained that she was a widow and had been at the Junction Inn, a pub kept by her son-in-law, when Whiston came in on the Friday of the crime sometime between midday and one o'clock.

This public house was (and still is, in 1988, though boarded up and derelict) in Queen's Cross, Dudley, on the main road about a half-mile from the bank where Meredith had gone to collect his firm's wages. It was at the end of his short-cut from Woodside to the works.

Sarah Humphrey's evidence shows a positive determination on the part of Whiston to follow and attack Meredith. She told the court that he had had something to eat and had drunk a pint of ale in the tap-room at the front, facing the street. 'He left and came back at about two o'clock and had another pint of ale. He asked me to take the blind down from the tap-room window that looked towards the church [St Thomas's] as he was looking for his sister. I let him do so. He left between two and three o'clock, putting the blind back.'

More was to be made of this later, but that was the case for the prosecution. However, Mr Harper, defending, asked the bench for an opinion on the matter of a sermon which had been preached concerning the case on the previous Sunday. He did not believe that it contained anything objectionable but, unless checked, it might lead to other expressions of opinion being given from the pulpit that might prejudice the prisoner. The Reverend Dr Cosens, vicar of Dudley from 1870 to 1892, thereupon announced his presence if required to give information and explanation, but the bench decided that they had nothing to do with events occurring outside. Nevertheless, more was to be heard of this cleric's preaching.

Meanwhile, the prisoner was committed for trial at Worcester Assizes.

As arranged, the resumed inquest took place at the town hall on that same afternoon, but no new evidence was forthcoming. However, a local newspaper dated 21 December revealed the contents of Dr Cosens' sermon, out of which Whiston's counsel vainly tried to make capital. The text was from the third chapter of the Book of Revelation: 'As many as I love I will rebuke and chasten. Be zealous, therefore, and repent ...' and so forth, at the end of which prayers were asked on behalf of the prisoner. The defence were certainly clutching at straws in rating this detrimental to a man who had such a weight of evidence against him and who had not denied his guilt.

The burial of Alfred Meredith at St Thomas' Church was attended by 150 workpeople from Hill & Smith, the works being closed as a mark of respect. It transpired that Meredith had trained a choir at a mission chapel at Netherton, and fittingly its members participated in the service.

His status now somehow upgraded to that of groom instead of horse-driver/labourer, Enoch Whiston appeared before Baron Huddleston (Sir J. Walter, 1815-90, a participant at the trial of the famous Rugeley poisoner, Dr Palmer) at Worcester on 21 January 1879, Mr Streeten and Mr Selfe prosecuting, and Mr Darling defending at the request of his lordship. The latter was to stress forceably that he did not stand there retained for the prisoner by his friends but was there simply through the kindness of the learned judge. This was an early form of legal aid, for it was felt that a man indicted for a capital offence must have representation.

Nothing new of significance was revealed by the prosecution. Mrs Lilly said that when she saw Whiston and Meredith they were going in the same direction, and the accused must have seen her; Daniel Round said that he had actually nodded to Whiston as he passed, but that Whiston '… took no notice, although I had worked with him for three or four years'.

Isaac Wall said under cross-examination that he was within sight of the place where the murder was committed, whilst the miner Thomas Smith actually saw Meredith fall, so that all in all the spot Whiston chose for his crime turned out to be nowhere near as lonely as he had supposed.

Mr Darling took the only course possible, attempting to cast doubt on Whiston's sanity. First he questioned Mary Terry about his headaches.

'Did he often complain of his head?'

'Yes,' Mary Terry replied. 'If I had gone by what my father said, I should not have gone with him, for he always said he was not right. He did not talk like a man who had his senses … he laid his head on the table for twenty minutes without saying anything.' She went on to say that Whiston's ear used to discharge sometimes, and he complained at such times of his head.

'Did he ever want to commit suicide?' Darling asked, and she replied that he had wanted to go and drown himself, and would have, had she not prevented him. 'That was once when we were going home about six yards from the canal.'

And this was the man she planned to marry!

In answer to the judge, Mary Terry said she had no quarrel with Whiston. 'He took his jacket off and gave it to me. If I had not pulled him back, he would have drowned himself. He seemed rather deranged. That was three months before his arrest.' No: she had not told anyone about it.

Chief Superintendent Burton, questioned on the same theme, admitted that the accused had once complained of a headache but, pressed by the prosecution, he agreed that the prisoner had spoken to him 'coherently at all times'.

Mr Darling now turned his line of attack upon the surgeon Goulder, referring to the discharge from Whiston's ear. Goulder said he had listened to the evidence concerning it, and said that it might arise from a cavity on the ear. 'I have read that insanity is sometimes caused by an abscess on the brain ... a man with an abscess on the brain is not likely to be in possession of his sound senses ... and when a man was suffering from a tendency to insanity, there was a disposition to suicide and homicide.'

This sounded good news for Whiston, but under cross-examination the surgeon had to concede that the discharge could proceed from other causes than abscess of the brain – most commonly from a cold.

Addressing the jury for the defence, Mr Darling said he would not deny that the prisoner had fired the pistol at Alfred Meredith: the question he would ask was whether the prisoner was mad or not at the time. 'What,' he asked, 'was the reason that caused the prisoner to take down the window-blind at the Junction Inn? It was to look for his sister', and he urged that, had he been on the lookout for the deceased, he would have stood up and looked over the blind.

Having sown this tiny seed of doubt, he turned to Mary Terry's story of Whiston's attempt at suicide and, having driven that titbit home, he submitted that the prisoner had never intended to kill Meredith. 'What he did was in a moment of temporary aberration, when he was not responsible for his actions.' He urged the jury to conclude that he had been unconsciously guilty of a crime and to bring in a verdict that Whiston had committed the murder when in an unsound state of mind.

In his summing-up the judge brought up all the facts that tended to show that there was reason in what the prisoner did. 'It would be most dangerous if a great crime were to pass unpunished because it was committed in a moment of aberration. The law in all cases presumes every man to be sane and possess a sufficient degree of reason until it was proved otherwise to the satisfaction of the jury.' He droned on in legal jargon, effectively demolishing the defence plea of insanity.

'The real question was, did he fire that pistol? If he did, then he was guilty of murder.'

The jury took half an hour to find Whiston guilty, and he was sentenced to death.

Insane? Perhaps not. But he must have been very simple-minded to shoot a man immediately after a former work-mate had nodded to him, and with several people around, not least PC Staines, only eighty yards from the scene. He must have known the area well. Had he forgotten about that engine-house hidden by a pit-mound? Also, could he really expect to shoot a man in the face and not kill him?

No one had seemed to query how he had come to obtain a pistol and ammunition, nor was any attempt made to discover from Whiston's sister if she had really been about to come past the Junction Inn at the time he was fiddling with the blind. His mother was not questioned either, even though he had claimed to have hidden money behind a brick in her pantry.

An appeal was launched on Whiston's behalf, as a result of which two 'medical men from London' visited him at Worcester Gaol by order of the Secretary of State, in order to make a report as to his sanity. Their report was not made public, but it could not have been favourable to Whiston, for the appeal failed.

Shortly before his execution, Whiston wrote to his family: 'I cannot help thinking about the miserable death which by my crime I have brought upon myself and which I so justly deserve. It breaks my heart to think that I have to go so soon; to die so early. I hope you will all feel contented for me to die, for I do myself, as it is true that I took the life of the poor young man Meredith.'

The execution took place at Worcester on 10 January; for some reason the gallows there had proved unsuitable, and a replacement was obtained from Northampton Prison. The deed was carried out in private, but some 500 people assembled outside and watched for the hoisting of the black flag to show that sentence had been carried out. The body remained hanging for an hour before it was cut down, and then the lowering of the flag signalled the end of the affair.

In retrospect it would seem that Enoch Whiston was a foolish, weak young man who was a victim of his time. Many were out of work – we do not know if he had left his employment, had been temporarily laid off or had been sacked – and the possibility of getting his hands on the large sum of money Meredith carried was clearly too much. At a time when the wage of an unskilled man was about thirteen-pence a day in today's coinage, it was surely wrong of Hill & Smith to permit a young chap like Meredith to collect his firm's wages unaccompanied, and moreover to make the journey at the same time each week so that his movements could be foreseen. Even today the movement of bulk wages presents a problem, and in the depression of the 1870s, not to provide a conveyance or escort was asking for trouble.

Evidence of the depressed state of trade is seen in a report published at the time of Whiston's execution, when the Amalgamated Association of Miners tried to get a penny a ton tax imposed on all coal raised in the UK for the purpose of a permanent relief fund. It didn't happen! The cost, it was said, would be too great, and besides, it would increase the cost of iron manufacture. At some future time (very vague) the matter ' ... might be entertained'.

To the credit of Enoch Whiston, he had apparently intended to 'do right' by his sweetheart Mary Terry, otherwise he would not have sped to her house and given her money. She in turn, under Mr Darling's direction, had done her best to free him of the noose.

8   The Corpse by the Pit Shaft, Bilston, 1914

A body is found with two bullet wounds on the right side of the forehead, and one in the left eye which had passed through the head – and for two days afterwards it was seriously being considered as suicide!

The scene is Bilston, now a part of Wolverhampton but in 1914 a separate borough, and it was in the district of Ettingshall to the west of Bilston town that the body was found on Tuesday 20 January, by two children on their way to the Springvale Works with their father's dinner (midday in the Black Country).

Springvale Works, the site of iron-making from blast-furnaces since at least the 1780s, was in 1914 operated by the Hickman family as Alfred Hickman Ltd, and Alfred (later Sir Alfred) Hickman had served as a mayor of Dudley. In 1921 the then vast complex was acquired by Stewarts & Lloyds, and steel continued to be made there, latterly under British Steel, until 1980, when the last furnace was blown out, marking the end of some 200 years of continuous production.

The area was never a place of solitude either by day or by night, and those children taking their father's dinner would be among probably hundreds similarly engaged, converging on the works, and indeed on other works all over the Black Country. In fact, it transpired that girls taking breakfasts to Springvale Works that morning had also noticed the body but had thought it to be merely a drunken man and had continued on their errand. After all, drunkenness was commonplace.

So the body lay surprisingly undetected all morning until the dinner-boys found it lying in a shallow cavity near the walled-up mouth of a disused pit shaft, of which there were a great many, for the heyday of mining the famous Ten Yard coalfield on which the Black Country stands – or rather stood – had long since passed, the emphasis switched largely to ironmaking.

When the police arrived and noted the injuries to the body, they found in a pool of blood four spent cartridges of what were described as the 'pin-fire' type, three live cartridges and a spent gun-cartridge. Later, there would be considerable controversy over these. The corpse was judged to be that of a man aged twenty to twenty-five years, and in his possession was found the sum of £9 2s. 3½d. in cash, a gold watch with a silver chain, a matchbox, a fountain pen and both English and foreign postcards, together with a letter.

The letter provided a vital clue to identity, for it was in an envelope addressed to Mr Kent Reeks, General Delivery, Boston, Mass., USA. The letter concluded, 'I remain your loving Granny Kent' and had been written to the dead man from 58 Chorley Road, Swinton, Manchester. Dated 24 December 1913, it dealt purely with domestic affairs, such as an illness in the family, and thanked the addressee for a Christmas card. It became clear that the addressee did not receive it in America, for the word 'Boston' on the envelope had been cancelled, and it had been readdressed to Liverpool post office.

It became obvious that the dead man, Reeks (as he proved to be), had been in Liverpool late on Monday 19 January and that he had collected the letter from a post office there, for it was postmarked 8.30 on the evening of the same day.

The immediate questions mooted were: why had the deceased left Liverpool for the Black Country? Had he travelled alone? What were his movements in and around

Bilston? And, of course, how had he come to meet his death on a pit mound? There were no signs of a struggle, but this, it was said, could be accounted for by the frozen nature of the ground.

A search failed to produce a revolver with which the wounds were inflicted, or the gun to which the spent cartridges belonged. Yet still the theory of suicide was aired!

Attention was paid to the pit-shaft, thought to be 450 feet deep, with about 250 feet of water, protected by a ten-foot-high brick wall rather than capped. It is interesting to reflect that such scant protection would be no deterrent to today's vandals, and one wonders if this was standard practice, bearing in mind the hundreds of similar worked-out pits sunk within the region. Even today householders are sometimes startlingly reminded of this when a hole appears in the garden, and when motorists find unexpected diversions because of a subsidence in the roadway.

Information began to filter through from Liverpool to the effect that a man named Reeks had stayed at a Temperance hotel in Lord Nelson Street close to Lime Street Station, on the Monday, and along with another man described as of 'seafaring type' who hailed from Chicago. The latter was said to be about thirty years of age, some five foot eleven inches tall, clean-shaven, dressed in a dark overcoat and wearing a bowler hat; he sometimes wore glasses. It was not known if the men were friends, business acquaintances or relatives, but they left the hotel on the same day, despite Reeks' having booked for three weeks. No deposit was paid.

Detectives visited Swinton, where Thomas Kent, an uncle of Kent Reeks, lived at 58 Chorley Road. He said that Reeks was a seaman, a fourth engineer with the United New Orleans Fruit Company, and held a second-class certificate. He had been born in Australia and had no settled home.

The uncle came to Bilston and identified the body as that of his nephew, thus removing any doubt, for there was always the remote possibility that the deceased had at some point found a letter addressed to Reeks and had placed it in his pocket. The various postcards seemingly gave no clue – perhaps they were souvenirs and not written upon.

'That's him, right enough,' said Thomas Kent, who revealed that he had seen Reeks on the previous Saturday when he had called on him. Reeks had travelled in *The Empress of Ireland* as a passenger from Boston and had spoken of it as '… the roughest passage I have ever made. Gales all the way.'

'Something had been said about Reeks' stopping at a Liverpool hotel with a friend from Chicago,' Thomas Kent commented. He added that his nephew had come to Britain only on a visit and was to have gone to his home in Australia in six weeks time. Reeks' mother had died in 1895, and the son was 'rather like her'. Asked if he had notified the father, he replied rather off-handedly that he had not, because he would be sure to read about his son's death in a Sydney newspaper. Hardly yet, since he had only just made formal identification!

Then came a revelation. After confirming that Reeks was aged twenty-four, Thomas Kent said that his nephew had shown him and his wife a wallet from which he had produced a $100 bill. He had others inside. 'He would have had a pretty penny on him, because he had been paid off from his boat at Boston immediately before sailing to England as a passenger. He told us that he preferred to carry paper money, it being safer than coin.'

It later became known that Reeks had had at least $500, which he kept in a dark green wallet. This fact was given national publicity, since any attempt to negotiate dollar bills in Britain would provide an important clue.

More disjointed information about Kent Reeks came to light. It was three years since he was last in Britain, sailing from Avonmouth. His last ship was the *Seconia*, of the United Fruit Company, Ohio. The uncle had a sister living in the tiny village of Swindon, near Dudley, just outside the Black Country, but asked, hopefully, if Reeks was likely to have been visiting her, Thomas Kent replied that his nephew would not even have known of her, so a possible reason for his being in the region bit the dust.

Back to Chorley Road, Swinton, this time to Mr and Mrs Richard Kent, whom Reeks had also visited on the Saturday night. They had been unable to put him up overnight, so he had returned to Liverpool, and indeed they had actually seen him off from Manchester Station that evening. This couple confirmed that Reeks had been in Liverpool to study for an examination with the objective of getting a British engineering certificate, since the Australian certificate was not so valuable. The examination was to have taken place in a few weeks, after which he had intended to return to Australia.

Richard Kent said that Reeks had been in no trouble, so far as they knew, and there was no girl. 'I had chaffed him on how many hearts he had broken since we saw him last, and he had replied, "I'll get married when I'm ninety." ' Yes: he had shown them a $100 bill and had told them there were others.

Mrs Sarah Kent, Reeks' grandmother, told of the letter she had sent him for Christmas. He had told them on the Saturday that he had not received it redirected from Boston – confirming that he had returned to Liverpool and collected it on the Monday.

It is interesting that virtually all Reeks' British relatives knew of his movements either by letters or by telegrams from him; even a branch of the family in the Potteries weighed in with confirmation. It was said that all his family were in '… good positions … his grandmother Kent was particularly fond of him … she had a substantial income and Reeks would always "be all right financially".'

The Liverpool police were on the track of a man who

had booked from Wolverhampton to Canada on a liner leaving Liverpool that week. Should it prove necessary, they said, 'Wireless communication can be requested and the man detained at the vessel's first port of call.' In the event, this mysterious traveller was the subject of considerable investigation on the other side of the Atlantic, as would later be revealed.

Various sightings of possible suspects came to nothing. On the Wednesday after the discovery of the body, a beetle scarf-pin was picked up close to the pit shaft. At first it was thought to be irrelevant, but when Thomas Kent was asked about it, he said that Reeks had had the pin in his possession when he had visited them.

Meanwhile, all manner of fanciful ideas were being put forward. It was even suggested that Reeks might have become acquainted with members of a pantomime company then visiting Bilston and intended to visit them, a theory based on nothing more substantial than the fact that this company had been appearing in Manchester the previous week. Reeks' family had stressed 'no girl'. Did the police find this hard to believe of a sailor?

By the time of the inquest at Bilston town hall on 22 January, the idea was growing that Reeks had travelled to the Black Country not by train but by car, a possibility that was to come to the fore several times, and not entirely discarded.

However, the inquest was confined to evidence of identity, and the jury were taken to the mortuary to see the bullet wounds and carefully note their respective positions in the victim's head.

The only witness called was the uncle, Thomas Kent, who repeated his story, declaring that he had himself put Reeks on a tram to Manchester, to get a train to Liverpool, on the Saturday at half past eight in the evening.

A surgeon attended the inquest but, after discussion with the coroner, left without taking part in the proceedings. The inquest was adjourned until 10 February.

A photograph of Reeks published in the newspapers resulted in information from a Manchester man, described as a railway official. 'I thought it could be the son of a lady my wife worked for before we were married.' He said that twenty-five years previously the deceased's mother had lived at Southport. She then went to Australia and married a man named Reeks. They had two children, and he felt certain that the victim was one of them, although he had never met him.

Why was he so sure? Because the photograph resembled the mother, and his Christian name was the maiden name of the mother. A good effort, but it did not help to catch the murderer(s)!

The vehicle theory was briefly enhanced when it became known that, according to a man employed by Wolverhampton Corporation, at about six o'clock on the morning of the murder a chauffeur-driven car had stopped and the driver had enquired of him the location of a 'certain locality in the town'. Motor cars were rare in 1914, and it should have been easy to trace. So it was, but, alas for hopes, it turned out to be a hired taxi in which a Manchester businessman was being driven to see relatives at Pensnet, near Dudley. A typical red-herring such as the police always encounter during investigations.

Captain the Hon. G. A. Anson, Chief Constable of Staffordshire, who was in charge of the case, visited Liverpool on 23 January to liaise with the police there, and it was discovered that revolver cartridges of a pattern similar to those that had caused Reeks' death had been purchased in Liverpool on the Monday morning of the day when he and his 'mysterious friend' had left the city.

'Two men came into the shop,' said the gunsmith. 'They asked for No. 32 cartridges for an automatic pistol. They bought fifty soft round cartridges and fifty solid cartridges, and the only remark being made was by the smaller man, who said, "That would put a cat out, wouldn't it?" ' referring to the soft-nosed cartridges.

'They were,' said the gunsmith, 'of a powerful kind. Bullets sold for an automatic pistol is not an ordinary event. I remember wondering at the time what they would be used for. The soft-nosed ones would make a ghastly wound. They are not often sold in this country.'

He described one man as being fairly tall, of medium build, clean-shaven, with a fresh complexion, dark hair and wearing a dark overcoat. He was aged about thirty. The shorter man was younger, also clean-shaven, wearing a light dust-coat.

Back in Wolverhampton, Captain Anson ridiculed the gunsmith's statement as being irrelevant, declaring that the cartridges found beside the body were very common .32 calibre, central fire. He also said that the police were not responsible for its having got around that they were described as 'pin-fire', and went on to remark, 'Four empty cases were found, and three cartridges unfired, but the latter, to all appearances, had misfired, as the caps were dented. The strange thing about all the cartridge cases was that they had been filed down, probably to fit an automatic pistol.

'There was no question of connecting the cartridges found with any particular make of pistol, but it was likely that an automatic pistol was used. It is practically certain that Reeks was killed with cartridges such as those found near him, and if he was killed away from the spot, the murderer must have collected the empty cartridges and strewn them around to give a pretence of Reeks' having killed himself or killed on the spot where he was found.

Adding that filing a cartridge was dangerous work, Captain Anson concluded what had amounted to a lesson in ballistics – of which the above account is only a part. He declared himself anxious to find the 'seafaring man from Chicago who stayed in the hotel in Liverpool at the same time as Reeks'.

Three weeks after the murder, by which time Reeks' body had been taken to Manchester and buried at St

Mark's Church, Worsley, the coroner's inquest was resumed. New evidence from Thomas Kent revealed that Reeks had said he had made the acquaintance of two girls aboard the ship to Liverpool. They were British, returning home for a holiday. He did not know where they lived.

Questioned about the beetle scarf-pin, Kent said that Reeks had shown it to them during his visit. This pin could not be found for the coroner's inspection, it having been sent to Liverpool to assist enquiries there, a fact that so annoyed that official that he threatened a further adjournment, but he was persuaded to think better of it.

The main witness now turned out to be Catherine Stanton, lodging-house keeper of 15 Lord Nelson Street, Liverpool. She told how the deceased had gone to her place on 17 January at around ten o'clock in the morning and asked for a room, saying he would stop for three weeks, and that he had come over on *The Empress of Ireland*. He said he was going to Manchester to visit friends, left after about ten minutes and returned later with a bag. He then went out for another bag, and while he was away another man came for a room for two or three nights. He signed the book J.H. Ramsden and said he came from Chicago. Questioned as to whether he appeared by his speech to be American, she answered, 'Many Americans do not speak with an accent.'

Ramsden had no luggage when he first arrived but had gone out and returned with a bag.

Catherine Stanton must have had her eyes wide open, for she was able to state that Ramsden was in his room when Reeks returned from Manchester and that they did not meet until breakfast, when it '… seemed that they had not met before'. She related how the pair had talked about the docks and seemed to get very friendly, Reeks showing Ramsden his discharge papers. They went out together early in the afternoon and again later in the day. Both men had arranged to be called at eight o'clock on the Monday morning (the 19th). They breakfasted together, after which Reeks went upstairs; when he came down again, he appeared surprised to find that Ramsden had gone out. He asked a maid which way he had gone and set off after him.

Stanton said that Reeks returned at about two o'clock and obtained some brown paper, which he took upstairs. Later he came down with a parcel bound with a leather strap. Reeks told her, 'Neither Mr Ramsden nor me will be in for tea.' He did not realize until she told him that Ramsden had paid his bill and evidently would not be back.

The police then stated that enquiries were being made for a tall, dark man, aged about twenty-eight, who had sent a telegram from Lime Street Station in Liverpool to Wolverhampton on 20 January at about eleven o'clock that night. He was described as five foot 11½ inches, clean-shaven, with dark hair and eyebrows, broad shoulders and a sailor's roll in his walk. His handwriting was almost illegible, and he was illiterate. No stone was being left unturned to find him, the coroner was assured, for it was believed that he had associated with Reeks in Liverpool.

Was this the mysterious Ramsden?

Having been told that the police of London, Birmingham and Staffordshire were in contact with the Liverpool police and that enquiries ranged from America to Australia, the coroner gave his summing-up. Despite all enquiries, he said, nothing decisive had been discovered, and nothing was known about the deceased from when he left Liverpool to when he was found at Ettingshall, Bilston.

The jury could have no doubt of cruel murder. Reeks must have been shot three times. He did not think any good could come of adjourning the inquest, and the only verdict the jury could reach was one of wilful murder against some person or persons unknown.

A juror asked if the man Ramsden had been traced – a

fact that he might well have deduced for himself – and was told no. The possibility of a motor car's having been used to dump the body was also raised by the jury but discounted on the grounds that a vehicle could not have got to the pit shaft, although a juror who knew the locality declared that there was a right-of-way across the land leading to Wright's foundry (Ernest N. Wright Ltd, adjacent to Hickmans' ironworks, also acquired later by Stewarts & Lloyds) which could have been used. The possibility of this track's having been used was not followed up by the coroner, who contented himself with a police assurance that the body did not appear to have been dragged.

A verdict of wilful murder was duly returned.

However, enquiries continued apace, and the Liverpool postmaster general was requested to place at the disposal of the police copies of all telegrams and telephone messages sent to Wolverhampton and Birmingham on 19, 20 and 21 January. It sounds a daunting task even in 1914 but was apparently technically possible, although nothing more was heard of this exercise apart from the fact that during the period in question two seafaring men with strong American accents had entered the Lime Street telegram office and sent telegrams to Wolverhampton, briefly stating that they would arrive with a friend.

Meanwhile, police in Liverpool and Canada were coming up with interesting information. Liverpool officers discovered that, when Reeks sailed in *The Empress of Ireland* from Halifax, Nova Scotia, he placed his valuables in an envelope provided by the purser. During the voyage he got 'chummy' with one of the Liverpool girls returning home, and he told her he had friends in Manchester and intended to visit them on the day he landed – which, of course, he did. He also said he had friends at Bournemouth and would see them before returning to Australia. When he retrieved his valuables, the girl (not named) saw bundles of dollar bills, the lowest being of $100 value.

On Saturday morning just prior to landing, Reeks told

the girl he had been very foolish the night before and had taken his coat off and thrown it on his berth, forgetting that the money was back in his possession. If we are to believe the girl, he said to her, 'I will just see that the money is all right now.' He pulled out an American wallet and, after looking at the notes, said they were correct. The girl said that there were a number of people about at the time he examined the wallet.

It seems almost as if Reeks wanted people to see his money, for, as we have heard, he also took the opportunity to flash $100 bills in front of members of his family. One may wonder why he had not examined his wallet in the privacy of his berth when he put his jacket on. Was it just a made-up tale to impress the girl?

Anyhow, the girl said that, when they left the vessel, Reeks put his baggage in a hotel and carried a suitcase. They walked to St George's Crescent, then she took a taxi-cab and went home.

Another aspect of police enquiries established that an emigrant had, on the night of 20 January, booked his passage from Thomas Cook in Lichfield Street, Wolverhampton, on the *Grampian* to St John's, New Brunswick (cost £6 5s.) in the name of Rogers. As this vessel neared St John's, a wireless message was received on board, and the man Rogers was questioned. When the news reached Wolverhampton, the police declared themselves ' ... satisfied beyond all doubt that he had not the slightest association with the case'.

A strange decision perhaps, since not many people were in the habit of booking to Canada from Wolverhampton in those days, and to do so on the very day of the murder was surely significant.

Rogers cannot have been questioned very thoroughly at sea, for the police had cause to reverse their opinion when, on 2 February, news from New Brunswick revealed that he had actually admitted to the St John's police that he knew Reeks.

'Where did you get acquainted with this man?' he was asked.

'In the hotel,' replied Rogers.

'Who was the third man in the hotel?'

'That doesn't matter.'

'Did you know this man had money?'

'Oh, he always had money.'

Asked when he had left the hotel, he said, 'The night the man was murdered.'

But on that night he had booked passage from Wolverhampton, so he could not have been in Liverpool. It was all most confusing, especially when it transpired that the man calling himself Rogers, who may or may not have been Ramsden, had several aliases – Joseph Rowland, for one. It was no doubt convenient to use surnames beginning with the letter R.

Now another twist. Despite his statement to the St John's police, Rogers now told everyone else he encountered that he had not known Reeks, and the Immigration Authorities said they had no further legal right to question him, although in their report they seemed far from satisfied. However, when Captain Anson saw the cablegram, he declared that in his opinion Rogers did not know Reeks, and he believed that he had only said he did in the first place in order that he might get sent back to Britain.

This is a hard deduction to follow, considering that he had only just left Britain and, as a suspect, would hardly wish to put his head in a noose!

It now came to light that Rogers had been staying with his sister, a Wolverhampton school-teacher, and when she learned that he had said he knew Reeks, she felt convinced that, if he *had* said it, '… it was in some measure due to his mind having become affected in some way.' It was she who had given him the fare, out of her savings, to go to Canada. 'He had searched in vain for work and was in trouble and distress.'

What trouble? She did not say.

When Rogers had told his sister on 19 January that he was in trouble, she said, they had agreed that the best thing he could do was to leave the country. After she had given him the money, he left for Stourbridge, where he spent the night, as confirmed by the police. He also spent the nights of the 17th and 18th in that town.

The name of Rogers' sister was not revealed, nor was she questioned further, but an account of Kent Reeks' movements in Liverpool, as painstakingly unearthed by the police there, indicates a pantomime of rapid movement. At about ten o'clock on the morning of 19 January he had arrived at a marine academy in South Castle Street; a half-hour later he was at a solicitor's office to swear an affidavit, after which he returned to the academy. By 11.40 he was again with his solicitor, leaving at noon. Whilst there, he said to the clerk, 'I have got to see a friend away to the Midlands.' This was the first intimation of Reeks' intention to visit the Midlands of his own free will.

At 12.45 he was yet again at his solicitor's, and from there he went once more to the academy. There he left a note: 'Please put the affidavit with my other papers. Keep them until I return, as I am going to Birmingham. I will be back about Thursday or Friday morning.'

Birmingham is some thirteen miles from the murder spot.

If the contents of the affidavit, and Reeks' papers, were studied for clues, nothing was published.

Time went on without further information of value coming to light. A host of questions remained unanswered. Why had Reeks, a seaman presumably needing all the experience he could get, signed off his ship at Boston and travelled to Britain as a passenger when he could surely have worked his passage and saved money, a commodity of which he seems to have been very fond?

Why did he not exchange his American currency on

arrival? He had flaunted dollar bills to relatives and on the boat; had he flashed them too carelessly elsewhere? Indeed, could a relative have done the deed, following him to Bilston and nipping smartly back home? Ah, but were not all the family in 'good positions'?

The ultimate mystery is why Reeks was at Bilston. Had his body been dumped there? Would the murderer – *could* the murderer – go to the gruesome trouble of carefully arranging the spattered brains which the police said were amidst the blood? Surely not!

National and international events swiftly removed the crime from the sphere of public interest. The Suffragettes were still militant following the death of their comrade Emily Davidson, who had shocked the country by throwing herself under the King's horse during the 1913 Derby, and now, in April, burned down Yarmouth pier. In July the King opened a conference on the Irish Home Rule issue, and shortly before, as the world knows to its cost, the Austrian Archduke Franz Ferdinand and his wife were assassinated at Sarajevo, indirectly sparking off World War I.

With so much in the offing, the death of Reeks fell into insignificance. Bearing in mind the heavy losses in merchant shipping sustained by the Allies due to U-boat activity, it is possible that his killer reduced Reeks' life by only a short time. One may conjecture also that, if his killer was indeed a seafaring man, he may soon have received retribution.

Postscript: *The Empress of Ireland*, the Canadian Pacific liner on which Kent Reeks sailed to Britain on his last voyage, was sunk on 29 May 1914 after colliding with a collier, *Storstad* in the St Lawrence River, in a bank of fog.

9 Triple Murder at Coombswood, Halesowen, 1878

Even in modern times, with its plethora of low-rise industrial estates and busy highways, Halesowen still retains a pleasant aspect, lying as it does in the valley of the little River Stour on the southern edge of the Black Country, but in 1878 it was exceedingly pretty, its collieries and factories well outside the village focal point of the parish church.

Despite the railway-building mania which began in the 1840s, Halesowen did not boast a railway station even at the beginning of 1878, although a line was under construction, and most of the industrial activity lay up from the valley floor to the north, about a mile distant, at Coombswood. It is here that in 1860 there began a works that was to become one of the largest manufacturers of steel tube in the world, conveniently sited on a canal which linked with the country's waterway network. Now the British Steel Company, it still exists, although much diminished.

During the nineteenth century and into the twentieth, workmen on day-shift had to be at their post by six or 6.30 in the morning, with the result that it was customary to have a breakfast break at nine o'clock. Because people rarely lived far from their place of work, men had their breakfast and other main meals brought to them by a member of the family, and it is this practice that launches us into our story.

At about 8.30 on the morning of 5 February 1878, Mrs

Phoebe Jones set off on her customary mission of taking breakfast to her husband, who was employed not at the tube works but at the Coombswood Brickworks. She heard the church clock strike nine as she returned from her errand and entered the two-up and two-down cottage which stood in a relatively lonely spot some distance from the turnpike road and which she shared with her family. As she became accustomed to the gloom of the interior, a horrible sight such as she would never forget met her gaze. Her daughter Amelia lay dead on the kitchen floor, along with her little granddaughter, Eve. Both had been attacked; their skulls had been broken, and blood was everywhere.

Nor was that all. On the bed upstairs her other granddaughter lay dying from similar injuries. No one else was in the house.

Phoebe Jones did not immediately think about Alice upstairs during those stunned moments that it took her to gather Eve's body in her arms and run outside screaming 'Murder!' at the top of her voice. Her cries were heard by a bailiff, Samuel Harris, of Coombswood Farm, who returned with her to the cottage, at which point Phoebe remembered Alice and dashed up the stairs to find the child lying unconscious in a pool of blood with terrible head injuries. She was still alive.

Chaos reigned as other folk arrived, and presently Phoebe's son James Jones, who lived locally, came hurrying to his mother's side. The police were notified, and Constable Peter Knowles hastened to the house, finding to his surprise that two men were already holding the man they firmly believed to be the killer – Joseph Harris, husband of Amelia and father of her two children. (But no relation to Harris the bailiff.)

Soon the whole of Halesowen was in an uproar as the gruesome details went the rounds. 'The brains were dashed out … Amelia's nose was almost severed.' There was no need to embroider the details. Meanwhile, Sam

Harris had toiled up the hill to fetch a doctor, hoping that at least Alice's life could be saved. Dr Walker accompanied him back from Blackheath and was at the cottage within the half-hour. By ten o'clock Dr Dunn from Halesowen was also present, but, sadly, both gave their opinion that Alice would not recover.

They were correct. She did not regain consciousness and died at two o'clock the following morning.

The coroner's inquest opened on the Wednesday afternoon, only to be adjourned for the jury to view the bodies. When it was resumed, on 1 March, at the New Inn, Halesowen, the sordid story of life in the cramped Harris household began to unfold. The police had by now satisfied themselves that Joseph Harris was their man, and he was brought from Worcester County Gaol by Superintendent Kemp of the Halesowen police.

Harris travelled by train to Hagley (one wonders why not Stourbridge, which was nearer and had a station on the same line) and was conveyed the rest of the way by road, with crowds lining the route, shouting 'Murderer!' and generally suggesting what ought to be done to him. According to the officer, Harris retained his composure during the twenty-two-mile journey, and throughout the inquest he was seen – courteously provided with a seat beside the pub fire – to listen intently but unmoved.

The first witness called was Phoebe Jones who told how she had left home on the morning of the crime leaving her daughter and three-year-old Eve in the kitchen. The prisoner, Amelia's husband, was sitting by the fire nursing Eve. Alice, aged seven, was still in bed. Harris had not spoken to any of them since he got up.

Having described her return and finding the bodies, she went on to paint a picture of life within the household. Her daughter and Harris, she firmly declared, had not lived happily together. Asked if she had ever seen a blow struck, she admitted that she had not, but, 'He used to threaten his wife and say what he would do. I could hardly make out his words, but anyway,' she added dismissively, 'it was all talk, his making threats. He had got it into his head that Amelia was unfaithful. It was jealousy.'

She said there had been no quarrel between the couple on the Monday morning, but there had been a '... terrible row the night before. I could hear them as I lay in bed and I put up with it until midnight, then shouted to them to be quiet so that I could get to sleep. They did shut up then.'

The next morning her husband had gone into their room and said to Harris, 'Now then, it's half past six. Time you were off.' Amelia had also said to him, according to her mother, 'Are you going to get up?' Then Amelia lit a candle and brought it to him, whereupon he blew it out, saying to her, 'I'm going to have a week's play' – meaning, in Black Country idiom, a week off.

Phoebe said she had told her son-in-law that he was not going to have a week's play. His father-in-law had to get up and go to work, and she was sure he would not encourage idle folk in his house. Nothing more was said, but Harris did reluctantly get up and, as already related, nothing more transpired before she left for the brickworks.

The witness then startled those not in the know by announcing that her son-in-law had been in a mental asylum. 'But only once. He had been discharged a fortnight after Rowley Wake the previous September.' No: Mrs Jones could not recall how long he had been in the asylum: she only knew that he had first been in a hospital, then at Winson Green institution, and from there transferred to the county asylum at Powick, a notorious place opened in the 1850s and closed, much changed, in 1988, situated between the city of Worcester and the Malvern Hills, beside the River Teme.

When he came out, Harris had returned to his family. According to Phoebe Jones, someone had told him whilst he was inside that his wife had become pregnant and had had a miscarriage. 'He accused Amelia of it some months after he came home.'

In answer to a question put by the coroner, Phoebe Jones said that she knew of the supposed pregnancy only from her daughter. Harris had said nothing about it to her. She had not heard infidelity mentioned during their many quarrels. As far as she knew, and she ought to know, the tale of the miscarriage was a lie.

She went on to relate how, on the Tuesday morning, as she was throwing a shawl over her head prior to leaving the house, Amelia had said to her, 'Don't be long, mother.' Her daughter had given no reason for making the request, but in hindsight she thought it significant. Harris, she declared, was ' … quick of hearing and would have caught the remark. It might have outraged him to think that his wife did not wish to be alone with him.'

An axe was produced in court, and Mrs Jones, greatly upset at sight of it, declared that it was one usually hanging on a nail in her kitchen.

Questioned by a member of the coroner's jury, she admitted that Harris had threatened to injure Amelia and that her daughter had told her several times that murder would be the ending of it.

Samuel Harris then gave evidence of having answered Phoebe Jones' cries, seeing the bodies and going to Blackheath for a doctor. At this point the coroner informed the prisoner that he might ask questions of the witnesses whose evidence he had heard, but he declined to do so.

Now the court learned how it was that Harris had been captured so quickly. James Jones, a grandson of Mrs Jones, said that on the Monday morning at about nine o'clock he had seen Harris close to Coombswood Farm, running away from his house. When he met up with him, he was taking his own father's breakfast and had to pass close to the Harris cottage. Harris had said to him, 'Your grandmother's gone with the breakfast. Don't go in. Make haste.'

It is likely that the lad had no intention of going in on the outward part of his errand, for breakfast timing was important and predominant in the minds of the carriers. Harris would have known that, if young Jones intended to call on his grandmother, he would do so on the way back, and to tell him not to go in then shows that his mind was befuddled. At all events, the lad went on his way.

Next to give evidence was Mary Ann Jones, wife of John Jones of New Buildings, Coombswood. At ten o'clock on the morning of the murders she saw Harris standing in a field. By then she knew what had happened, and shouted to Harris, 'What have *you* been doing?' to which he replied, 'Doing what? I've done nothing.'

She said to him, 'There's Amelia and the two children lying in the house.' He replied, 'I'll go to 'ess. Let me go and see her.' (A juryman explained that ' 'ess' was a slang word for ashes, but even so the remark did not make sense unless Harris was implying that he would burn in Hell.) Anyhow, Harris stood where she had spoken to him and made no attempt to return to his home.

Questioned, Mary Ann said she had not seen any blood on Harris' clothing, although there might have been. She added that she did not know of any reason why Harris and his wife should not have lived happily together, but conceded that there '… were rumours about'.

Now another Jones said his piece: Adam, Amelia's brother. He had slept at the cottage the night before the murders and had heard no quarrel until about half-past six on the Tuesday morning. Here he affirmed the argument which had taken place about Harris' refusal to get up and go to work, insisting on a week's 'play'. He did get up at eight o'clock, and when Adam left for work, Harris was cutting some tobacco. He said nothing to him.

Young Adam went on to relate that on the Monday night Harris had taken a pair of trousers and a waistcoat to a pawnbroker at Blackheath, where he had bought them the week before. Why this fact should be thought to have any significance was not made clear, but it does serve to show the poverty-stricken way in which working-class people clothed themselves, purchasing clothing that some even poorer soul had been unable to redeem. The attraction of the three brass balls was like a magnet in industrial areas of the Black Country right up to World War II.

Adam thought Harris had taken the clothes back because they were too large. Questioned by the jury, he had said he had never heard Harris use threats towards his wife, although he had lived with them since Harris came home from the asylum.

Samuel Parkes, next to give evidence, said he had seen Harris about a hundred yards from his own place on the morning of the murder. He had seen a man named Silas Plant grab Harris by the coat and had gone over to them, saying to Harris, 'What have you done the murder for?' Harris had denied being responsible. There was no further conversation as he and Plant held on to their prisoner until PC Knowles arrived and took him into custody.

Two men named Timyns and Toy, and another man named Palmer, fetched a clothes line from a cottage garden and bound Harris with it. There was no struggle, and from the time of the murder Harris had made no serious attempt to escape.

PC Knowles said that, when the prisoner was taken back into his cottage, he merely glanced at the body of his wife, '… without apparent comprehension … There was blood on the trousers and shirt-sleeve of the prisoner.'

Superintendent Kemp then described how he had found Amelia Harris lying on the floor with her feet towards the window. She was bleeding from wounds and there was blood on the floor. The child Eve lay on a seat, and upstairs he found Alice lying on the left side of the bed. There was a lot of blood. Searching the house, he discovered a number of tools in a recess in the kitchen. Among them was the axe, wet as if dipped in water and only partly dried. There was blood mixed with the water.

This was hardly surprising, for Harris would scarcely have had time to clean the axe, having had to carry out the whole grisly deed in barely a half-hour.

Kemp told Harris that he would be charged with the murder of his wife and the child Eve, and with maliciously wounding the other child, Alice. The next morning, when Kemp heard that Alice was dead, he told him that he would be charged with her murder also. The next day Harris was taken to Worcester Gaol, and as he was escorted through the streets and passed over a canal bridge, he told the officers, 'I've been this way before. I know the road. It was when I was going to Powick, and we came back this way. That is why we often quarrelled. When we had a few words, my mother-in-law and Amelia used to vex me by saying that they would send me to Powick again.'

One imagines that such talk would do rather more than 'vex'. If true, it was asking for trouble. In fact, it was the worst thing his family could do, for the fear of being sent back to the asylum would be overwhelming. In those times mental illness was not properly understood, and to have been an inmate of a lunatic asylum was shameful; it was avoided at all costs.

Harris continued to chat during the journey. He asked when he was to be tried, and was told that no date had yet been fixed. Having mused on this for a time, he said, 'I think it would be best for me to say nothing at all, wouldn't it? Leave them to say as much as they like.'

Following Kemp's evidence, Mr Dunn, a Halesowen surgeon, detailed the injuries inflicted on Mrs Harris. She had five wounds on her head and face, one in the centre of her forehead which had passed through the bone to the brain. There was a compound fracture of the nasal bone, a lacerated flesh wound over the left eyebrow, and others to the right temple and lower lip; her teeth had been knocked out and jaws fractured.

It was apparently not thought necessary to disclose the

injuries to the children, but the surgeon thought that all might have been inflicted by the axe produced.

In his summing-up the coroner expressed regret that, according to the medical evidence, there was no means of determining by analysis whether the spots of blood found on Harris' clothing were human or not. 'If they were those of a human,' he told the jury, 'the fact would go a good way to establishing the case against the accused. If they were not, a strong suspicion against him would be removed.'

Was that so important, considering the weight of the evidence? Anyhow, it was of negative help to the jury, who after only a brief retirement returned to declare Joseph Harris guilty of murder.

These were stirring times nationally, and whilst Harris awaited trial at the Lent Assizes the literate would have been more interested in reading of Britain's world role at the very peak of its Empire on which the sun never set (folk living in the industrial gloom of the Black Country might well have felt that it never rose!). Only two years earlier Queen Victoria had been proclaimed Empress of India, and, moreover, Her Majesty had started once again to live a public life after years of seclusion following the death of her 'dearest Albert'. Yet even she was to be shattered anew, in this year of Harris' crime, by the death of her daughter Alice, who died on the very anniversary of her father's death after nursing her children through diphtheria.

Harris came up for trial at Worcester on 20 March, and right at the outset the presiding judge, Lord Justice Baggaley (1816-88, MP for Hereford 1865-8, knighted 1868), addressed the jury concerning the 'crime of murder that would be placed before them', saying that the defence on the prisoner's part would be that he was of unsound mind at the time of committing the murders.

Although indicted for the murder of his wife and two

children, Harris was charged in the first count of murdering his wife. Mr Self prosecuted, the defence being handled by Mr Plowden and, to the surprise of most people, considering that the prisoner had already been more or less written off as insane, the case lasted for very nearly five hours.

Phoebe Jones revealed that in October 1876 Harris had been in the General Hospital, Birmingham, for a month, after which he was taken to the asylum at Winson Green, and in March 1877 was removed to Powick Asylum. He was discharged in October of that year. She did not know why he had been placed in these institutions, nor was anyone asked the reason.

For about six weeks Harris had lived with his family peaceably, but in consequence of tales concerning his wife's infidelity things had been 'less than harmonious'.

Cross-examined by Mr Plowden, she said she did not know if Harris had come from Powick Asylum cured or if he was on treatment. She did not know if any instructions had been given by the 'medical men' for treatment. He had seemed well before he was taken to the General Hospital. After he became suspicious of his wife, Phoebe had repeatedly told him that there was no truth in the rumours he had heard. His wife had likewise assured him, but he had continued to make accusations.

Phoebe Jones probably knew more than she admitted, for Amelia would surely have related to her every little detail, even if no one else did, tittle-tattle (gossip) always being rife in Black Country communities.

Plowden: 'Did you ever remind him that he had been in a lunatic asylum?'

Mrs Jones: 'I did not. He said he had never been in an asylum.'

'Had you ever threatened to send him there?'

'I never have.'

'Have you ever told him he ought to go back?' Plowden persisted.

'My daughter had, not me,' she answered reluctantly.

Plowden seized on this. 'Was it on the occasions when he spoke about Amelia being unfaithful that she said she would send him back to the asylum?'

'It might have been,' Phoebe Jones replied, and she went on to add that on the morning when her daughter had asked her to return soon, it was because she was afraid of her husband. 'He seemed suspicious in his manner.'

Yet she had not been deterred. Such was the importance of routine and the beholden duty of a wife that, come rain or shine, even with a hint of violence to a daughter, the breakfast must reach the husband on time at his workplace.

Adam Jones, Amelia's brother, next took the stand and told how, since Harris had returned from the asylum the previous October, he had worked only five days at the pit. Why? Was he inefficient, a danger to other folk underground or just plain lazy? No pit manager was called to explain, and Jones went on to say that Harris had put in 'some time as a nailer in a nearby workshop'.

As everyone in court from the judge down well knew, half-hearted nail-making was no good; it had to be at least a ten-hour stint day after day, and even small children soon learned the trade, working alongside their parents. So this revelation clearly established Harris as being unable to pull his weight in the poverty-stricken times in which they lived. He therefore had to be fed and clothed after a fashion, being nothing short of a burden. In no way could the poor chap, with his mental history, ever be the flavour of the month, and his father-in-law's attempt to get him out of bed on the morning of the murder reflects the frustration he aroused.

Various witnesses trooped into the court to repeat their earlier evidence, and a statement made shortly before by the prisoner was admitted. In effect it said that at a Christmas party at the house a quarrel had arisen between himself and his wife. She had reminded him of his confinement at Powick.

New evidence was given by Mr J. Sherlock, superintendent at Powick Asylum. He said that Harris had been admitted on 20 March 1877 as a dangerous lunatic. On October 18 he was discharged on trial. At the end of October he was finally discharged on a certificate from the Powick medical officer. 'It was the usual thing,' he told the court, 'when madness was returning, for a married man to have suspicion of his wife's infidelity. When in the asylum, a general suspicion all round was noted. Such a suspicion was likely to result in injury to the person suspected. He would also be likely to kill others implicated. The cool behaviour of the prisoner following the tragedy would lead him to doubt his sanity.'

'Assuming a person to have been in an asylum for twelve months,' he went on, 'and whilst there to have exhibited the symptoms mentioned, he [Sherlock] would be suspicious of such a person's sanity if he heard of his committing a murder within a few months of his discharge.'

The judge kindly forbore to enquire why, in that case, Harris had been released and given a final discharge.

Mr Self then briefly summed up for the prosecution, commenting on the fact that there were no signs of insanity on the part of the prisoner noted by the 'medical men' when they were called to attend the deceased.

That was the case for the prosecution.

For the defence, Mr Plowden urged that the prisoner was of unsound mind at the time of the murder, a fact which most present would have long realized. Thus it did not take the jury long to return a verdict of 'not guilty on the grounds of insanity'. The judge then said that Harris would be kept in custody during Her Majesty's pleasure.

Despite the awfulness of his crime, one can feel some sympathy for Joseph Harris. The superintendent at Powick was being very wise after the event, and after all

Harris actually had in his possession a signed piece of paper to say that he was sane! He had undoubtedly been taunted by his wife and others. He was a failure and useless. In the end it was all too much, and there was the axe conveniently hung on the wall.

Postscript: A search of the records of Powick Asylum, now deposited at the Medical Records Office, Newtown Hospital, Worcester, confirms the date on which Harris was said to have been admitted. However, it was on 5 November 1877 that he received his discharge certificate. He is described in the records as ' ... feeble and in a precarious condition, and had great difficulty in breathing. Otherwise he was quiet and gave no trouble.'

After the trial he did not return to Powick. It is thought that he was sent to Broadmoor.

10 Dastardly Maiming of Horses and Cattle, Great Wyrley, 1903

February 1903: two horses found in a field on different days with their bellies ripped open. April: another horse similarly maimed. May: a cow, horse and sheep maimed. June: two cows and two sheep likewise. Then on 17 August came the maiming of a horse whilst the fields were crawling with police patrols drawn from all over the Black Country, sparking off a story that had wide-ranging ramifications.

The inhabitants of the Staffordshire village of Great Wyrley, where it all began, just beyond the eastern fringe of the Black Country, were horrified and fearful of events beyond their comprehension. The shock-waves spread across the whole of the Black Country and eventually attracted national interest, involving none other than Sir Arthur Conan Doyle, creator of the great detective Sherlock Holmes.

No human murder here, but threats of same. It all started with a wedding present way back in 1874, and that is where we must begin a tale that set the country alight and rumbled on through the decades until the First World War.

Exactly how it came about we do not know, but in 1874 a Miss Stoneham met and married the Reverend Shapurji Edalji, a Parsee who had converted to Christianity as a boy in Bombay – Parsees being descendants of Persians who had fled to India in the seventh and eight centuries to escape Moslem persecution and who still retained their religion. But becoming a Christian did not change the colour of Edalji's skin – hence the trouble that was to ensue.

Miss Stoneham's uncle held the gift of the living of Great Wyrley, and gave it to the couple as a wedding present.

It is not difficult to imagine the impact of a coloured vicar's taking over a rural church at that time, when we still have widespread colour prejudice over a century later. The congregation and non-church folk alike must have been appalled, and derogatory words such as we are not supposed to use today were freely spoken. Yet the good Reverend and his wife sat tight, and two years later they gave birth to a son, christened George.

Hostility continued, boiling over in 1888 with a spate of anonymous letters sent to Edalji. Hate-messages were scrawled on his garden wall, and when a servant girl who worked at the vicarage, Elizabeth Foster, was discovered to be the culprit, she was hauled before the magistrates and bound over to keep the peace.

Four years later there were more anonymous letters, attention switching to George Edalji, now sixteen years of age. One letter said: 'I swear by God I will murder George Edalji soon. The only thing I care about in this world is revenge. Sweet revenge I long for. Then I shall be happy in Hell.'

Another letter said: 'May the Lord strike me dead if I don't murder George Edalji!'

Strong stuff! What was the lad supposed to have done?

At about the same time a number of pranks were played on the vicar. Cartloads of goods not ordered began to arrive on the doorstep; notices appeared saying that the vicarage was to let, and to the effect that the vicar would be pleased to arrange meetings between ladies and eligible bachelors.

Neither the vicar nor his wife took this kind of harassment seriously. After all, they were well used to unpopularity, although how the Reverend managed to carry out his parish duties under the circumstances taxes the imagination. He certainly did not report these hoaxes to the police, aware perhaps that he would receive little sympathy from that quarter.

Now comes the odd incident of the key to Walsall Grammar School, a massive, old-fashioned key, found one day on the vicarage doorstep and handed to the police by the Reverend himself. The matter reached the ears of the Chief Constable of Staffordshire, and young George was blamed. But he did not attend Walsall Grammar School and had not been in Walsall, he declared, for a month beforehand. It was one more mystery to add to a growing catalogue destined to take a more sinister turn.

Another letter to the vicar: 'Before the end of the year your kid will either be in the graveyard or disgraced for life.'

Anyone who knew George Edalji, and who was not blinded by prejudice because his skin was darker than that of other local youngsters, knew him to be shy and reserved and (not surprisingly) of a nervous disposition. He suffered defective eyesight and wore very strong spectacles, yet he was nobody's fool and so applied himself to his studies that he won a scholarship and set his sights on becoming a solicitor. This he did, becoming clerk to solicitors E. C. Osbourne & Co, Birmingham, to which city he travelled daily by train. His eventual triumph in becoming a respected lawyer would be a further cause for fury amongst those who detested the Edalji family.

However, between 1896 and 1902 the anonymous letters ceased and a degree of normality existed. After all, and despite the nearness of a colliery, Great Wyrley was a pleasant village in which to live. Then, in 1903, the animal maimings already mentioned began, lasting spasmodically from February to June, always at night and always horrific in the injuries inflicted.

Anonymous letters started afresh, not to the vicar as

before but to George, now aged twenty-eight. They were insulting and frequently accused him of being the maimer of cattle. Sometimes the letters went to the police, and one such, passed on to George and signed 'Lover of Justice', declared that, although he, the writer, didn't like 'natives', he didn't think George Edalji had anything to do with the maimings. 'People all say it is you because they think you are the right sort. Go away and you will be suspected no more.'

One postcard even referred to the Elizabeth Foster incident of 1888, saying, 'Why don't you go on with your old game of writing on walls?' George had been only twelve at that time.

A routine of exchanging these anonymous letters evolved, George handing his to the police and vice versa. One such, handed over by the police, must have knocked him for six – it was written on the headed notepaper of his own firm, Osbourne & Co. Dated 18 July and addressed to a PC Robinson, it read: 'You daren't lock me up. You great cowardly brute ... I will murder you if you are not careful how you behave. I will shoot you with my father's gun through the head if you come my way or go sneaking to any of my pals.'

This so worried George that he had an advertisement placed in a local paper offering a reward of £25 for information leading to the conviction of anyone circulating rumours or anonymous letters concerning him. No replies were received, and the police merely regarded this as further indication of George's cunning.

Then, on 17 August, a horse belonging to the Great Wyrley Colliery Company was maimed. It was the last straw, tweaking the noses of the watching police.

On the morning of 18 August Inspector Campbell found the chestnut-coloured pony with its belly ripped open. He also discovered footprints leading from the dead animal to a public footpath, and although the footprints did not show on the harder ground, it was clear, at least to his mind, that they would have continued in the direction of the vicarage.

Campbell had a long memory and regarded George as a thief and liar over the business of the grammar school key twelve years earlier. He had felt no hesitation in going straight to the vicarage, knowing full well that George would be at his office in Birmingham, and had interviewed the startled Reverend and his wife. Although he had no right to do so, having no search warrant, he asked to search the house, and the much maligned vicar saw no reason to refuse. Imagine the inspector's delight when he found in George's bedroom a suit with bloodstains on the sleeve, and a number of hairs which he immediately assumed came from a horse. Also in the bedroom he found a cut-throat razor also stained with blood. To clinch the matter to his satisfaction, he found a pair of boots that were wet, as well they might be in a rural area in February.

With no more ado, the inspector boarded a train to Birmingham and bearded George in his office, having sent the bloodstained jacket for expert examination. George Edalji was flabbergasted. Yes: he knew that the suit was bloodstained. It had been for some time. As for the horsehairs, if such they were, he could have picked them up anywhere, perhaps simply by leaning against a gate or fence where a horse had rubbed itself.

And the razor? 'Stained for weeks,' said George.

No matter, Inspector Campbell charged him then and there, with maliciously maiming and wounding a horse belonging to the colliery company, despite George's insistence that on the night in question he had taken a pair of shoes to be mended, leaving home at about eight o'clock and returning at about 9.30. He had had his supper and gone to bed in a room he shared with his father.

George's appearance at the local police court created a sensation, many people feeling that at last they had the Edaljis where they wanted them. His parents and friends were present to lend support, and a Mr Meek was engaged for the defence – not perhaps an inspiring name under the circumstances, when strength and forcefulness were needed. However, he did his best. The evidence against his client was slight, and he asked that, if a formal remand was taken, his client be released on bail under his parents' surety. Mrs Edalji, he said, had a separate estate of her own. Moreover, the prisoner's business in Birmingham was being ruined.

The bench allowed bail with reluctance in a sum of £200 from the prisoner, his mother lodging £100, his father £100, and also an outside surety of another £100 – the magistrates intended to make it as tough as possible. But to everyone's astonishment George refused bail and was sent to Stafford Gaol. His legal mind had been working over-time, and his decision was a calculated gamble, even though it meant a stay in gaol of two months. As we shall see, it worked – but not to his advantage.

At the police court hearing, it had transpired that, on the night in question and for many nights previous, the inspector had had over twenty policemen patrolling the fields and had even had the vicarage surrounded, drawing officers from all over the region. Why then had none of them seen George leave the vicarage at the time when the horse-maiming was judged to have occurred, probably between two and three in the morning? That was easy to answer. Edalji possessed all the inbred cunning of his dark-skinned brethren: he was dark, it was a dark night, and besides he probably knew a secret way out of the vicarage. Anyway, after several nights of tedious watching, some of the constables may not have been sufficiently vigilant.

What about his father, a respectable man of the cloth, swearing that his son, with whom he shared a bedroom, had not left the house? He would say that, wouldn't he?

More difficult to explain was the fact that the hairs on George's suit did not belong to the dead horse after all.

Too bad! Never mind, though: his boots fitted the marks in the soft earth of the field. Ah, but in his eagerness to nail his man the inspector had omitted to have casts of the footprints taken, and since then the feet of dozens of curious sightseers had gone over the ground. However, several sets of prints still fitted George's boots, and Campbell said he would have no hesitation in declaring that he had traced the footprints and identified them as those of Edalji. He did so without batting an eyelid.

Even when a veterinary surgeon gave it as his opinion that the injuries to the horse had not been committed with a razor, but probably with a knife, Inspector Campbell had not been deterred, not even after twelve constables had dug up the vicarage garden! That nothing was found merely implied that 'the cunning fellow' had found a safe hiding-place for the weapon. Anyway, perhaps some of the earlier maimings had been done with a razor. Who could say now?

Nothing was going to deter Inspector Campbell from making his charge stick, and, as we have seen, George Edalji was committed for trial at Stafford, refusing bail in the meantime.

Then, whilst he was safely under lock and key – sensation! On the night of 21 September another horse was maimed. Although a shattering blow to the police and the community, it was precisely what Edalji had gambled on in refusing bail. Surely they would now accept that he was innocent?

Nothing of the kind.

The horribly mutilated animal that was the victim of this latest atrocity was found early in the evening of the following day by one John Jayes, a miner at the local pit. He had been going along a lane connecting with the main Walsall road when he saw portions of the entrails of the animal, which had been completely disembowelled. It proved to be a well-bred six-year-old horse, the property of Harry Green, a member of the Walsall Troop of the

Staffordshire Yeomanry. Purchased for military purposes, it was valued at £40.

This was the ninth occasion on which animals had been killed in the area, and it was confirmed that the injuries inflicted were similar to the other outrages. Alarm spread through the district, for people had lulled themselves into a sense of security with George Edalji firmly under lock and key. It had not been considered necessary to continue police surveillance of the countryside, and now people fearfully reminded themselves of the contents of one of the anonymous letters read out during the court proceedings: 'During the coming winter attacks will be made upon children, and they will be served in a manner similar to the cattle.'

The Reverend Edalji and his wife were, of course, delighted at this latest maiming and sent a triumphant message to their son. This was a vindication of his character. 'We hope before long to be able to prove it before all the world. We are thankful now that you refused bail. It was a cruel ordeal for the family.'

National newspapers now began to devote space to the Wyrley maimings, and the police authority offered a reward of £50 for information leading to an arrest. On the following Monday night a public meeting was held to consider what action parishioners might take, and a committee was appointed to suggest a scheme for raising subscriptions to compensate the owners of the dead animals. An opinion was expressed that, if those present could lay hands on the perpetrator, it would be 'God's mercy on him'. Various speakers really let fly, but a mercenary note crept in when it was pointed out that it might be the object of the perpetrator to inflict serious financial loss upon the owners of the animals. If that was so, and compensation was arranged, it could prove a very costly business.

The idea that the locals lived in fear was pooh-poohed, the chairman declaring that he '… did not believe any man, youth or boy was afraid.'

What about the women? He appeared to have forgotten another anonymous letter that had been read out in court. 'When the dark nights come in towards November I will serve twenty wenches the same way.'

Despite the vicar's hopes, the trial of his son went ahead, opening at Stafford on 20 October and lasting an astonishing 3½ days. It was held not before a judge at the assizes but at the Quarter Sessions before a local landowner who was appalled at the maiming of animals and seemingly had little sympathy for the accused. Mr Disturnal and Mr Harrison prosecuted; Mr Vachell and Mr Gandy defending. The most minute details were examined at great length, much being made of the bloodstained clothing, the condition of the razor, and the prisoner's supposed movements on the night of 17 August, when he had gone to the shoemaker.

George Edalji told the court that, on his way back, being a bit early for supper at half-past-nine, he had walked on past the vicarage as far as Green's farm but had not gone inside. This was unfortunate, since it was Green's horse that had been maimed whilst he was in gaol, and Green's son had already confessed to having done it. This led to the idea that there was a gang of maimers at work, a theory strengthened by subsequent events.

Young Green was not called as a witness, the chairman saying that, had he been called, it would not have been possible to ask incriminating questions, and it was useless to have in the witness-box a person to whom only certain questions could be addressed. 'There is no evidence to believe that Green's motive was spite, or evidence of his mental insanity.'

So it was all right for young Green to maim a horse but not Edalji. Double standards? Had strings been pulled?

The anonymous letters occupied a great deal of time, twelve being read out in full, posted from various Black Country towns including Wolverhampton, Darlaston and Wednesbury. Edalji proved that on the day on which one of the letters had been posted he and his sister had gone on a trip to Aberystwyth, leaving at five in the morning and not returning until midnight.

So what? Someone could have posted it for him!

The shoemaker, John Hands, confirmed that George had brought shoes for repair on the evening of 17 August. He had been wearing a blue suit 'something like an officer's uniform' and not the one seized by Inspector Campbell bearing blood and horsehair.

A small plus-factor for the prisoner!

The Reverend Edalji then told how he shared a bedroom with his son, who could not have gone out without his knowing, for he did not sleep well, and anyway the door was locked. Eyebrows were raised. 'Why,' he was asked, 'did two grown men find it necessary to lock themselves in their bedroom?' 'It was the custom,' was the simple reply.

His wife, Charlotte Elizabeth Stuart Edalji, was then called, and she told how she had brought downstairs all her son's clothes at the request of Inspector Campbell. This was at variance with the inspector's reported statement earlier, that he had gone up to the vicarage bedroom. She was not sure which suit her son had worn on the night.

For his part, George Edalji firmly denied writing the letters or maiming animals, and described his movements on the night of 17 August in great detail, adding nothing not already known. (It is interesting that, only five years before, in 1898, the Criminal Evidence Act had been passed, allowing prisoners to give evidence in their own defence. That is why in none of the earlier cases dealt with in this book were prisoners called to speak for themselves. They had merely been invited to ask questions at the discretion of the judge.)

When every ounce of evidence had been presented, there was heightened expectancy when, on the fourth day, Mr Vachell began his speech for the defence. As on previous days, the public galleries were filled, mainly by ladies 'well provided with lunch baskets'.

Vachell discounted the evidence of various witnesses who claimed to have seen George Edalji on the evening of 17 August because their evidence did not tally and he could not have been at all the places mentioned at the times given; also he questioned why the watching police seemed not to have seen all these people, or at any rate had not stopped and questioned them. He dismissed the possibility that Edalji might have got up in the night and committed the deed, and rejected the relevance of the stains on the clothes – just two spots which, according to the evidence of a doctor, were old stains. As to the horsehairs, there was doubt as to where they came from, the prisoner's parents had declared on oath that there were no hairs on his clothes.

Referring to the letters: 'Were the jury going to say in a criminal case, when the prisoner's whole future was at stake, that they would act solely on the experts' opinion? Many anonymous letters had been received in the district since the prisoner was arrested, and for all the court knew they might have been in the handwriting said to be the prisoner's.'

Vachell complained about the absence of Green. 'They knew from the police that he had killed a horse by ripping it up in much the same manner as the horse on 17 August, and they had a man at large who admitted having done it. Why,' he demanded, 'should the police say therefore that the prisoner was guilty? Had the prosecution suggested a motive? If these things were not done for spite, the only other explanation was that the person who did them was in some way insane.

'Did the jury think the prisoner, whom they had by now had under observation for three days, was of unsound mind?' They might rest assured, he told them, that the medical officer at Stafford Gaol would have been called to give evidence had he found the slightest suggestion of insanity.

However, perhaps the most hard-hitting statement put forward by the defence was that, 'The police had made up their minds how the crime was done, and had only put forward that evidence which supported that theory.'

It was a good try, Vachell's speech lasting for two hours, but the prosecution came back strongly, and at the end of it all George Edalji was found guilty and sentenced to seven years penal servitude. Date: 23 October 1903. But his conviction was nowhere near the end of the story.

After twenty-seven years of largely bitter opposition, the Reverend Edalji resigned the living of his parish. Maiming outrages continued for a further six months and then ceased – for some years.

The Edalji case had occupied the news for so long that other events tended to go unheeded, although housewives would have become aware of a shortage of farthings (one quarter of an old penny) because of the rise in the price of bread to an awkward 2¾d. a loaf, and the mint had not produced a sufficiency of this small coin to meet demand. (Even in 1935 a single farthing was still worth having, for it enabled poor children at a London school to obtain a breakfast at a Salvation Army Centre – hot cocoa, bread and jam, and porridge.)

But to continue with the Edalji saga. Two days after his trial ended, a new character appeared on the scene, sending a batch of anonymous mail and signing himself 'G. H. Darby, Captain of the Wyrley Gang'. Darby's first letter was to George Edalji in prison and asserted Edalji's innocence, but thereafter he appeared to jump onto the criminal band-wagon that rolled locally for the next twelve years. Whether he was simply mischievous, deliberately raising false clues to harass the police, or had inside information – police were once called 'Darbies', from an old slang word for 'handcuffs' – or whether he was himself the maimer, was never discovered, and his identity remained a mystery.

So frequent were Darby's letters and postcards, mainly to the local press, that he seemed always to be in the news and, as if under his orchestration, maimings eventually resumed, though trival enough not to cause serious injury to the animals.

However, in August 1907 a horribly mutilated horse died, and where else but at Great Wyrley?

Darby intimated that he knew all about this, and about even later crimes such as the murder of Kent Reeks in January 1914 (see Chapter 8).

Over the years Darby continued to send postcards by the score on all manner of crimes of which he claimed knowledge, and these were posted in towns all over the region: West Bromwich, Willenhall, Tipton, Dudley, Wednesbury and even Birmingham. Rightly or wrongly, the mysterious Darby became linked with George Edalji, especially when Sir Arthur Conan Doyle was commissioned by the *Daily Telegraph*, in 1906, to put on his Sherlock Holmes hat and investigate the whole business.

Before that, there had been grave disquiet at Edalji's sentence. Possibly it was the British way of siding with the underdog, but after his conviction opinion tended to swing in his favour – though not in Great Wyrley. For example, a Mr R. D. Yelverton, formerly chief justice of the Bahamas, took an interest in the case and organized a petition. Over 10,000 signatures were obtained, including those of 'hundreds of lawyers and some KC's. The influential paper *Truth* carried articles on the case.

George Edalji served three years of his sentence, while evidence was being accumulated based on Conan Doyle's endeavours to obtain for him a free pardon. Conan Doyle visited the scene of the maimings and declared that the authorities had made a serious blunder in the beginning by arresting the wrong man.

'I analysed the facts,' Conan Doyle wrote in a pamphlet

published in 1914, 'and showed, I think, to the satisfaction of any impartial man, how idiotic had been the verdict of the Staffordshire jury which had sent this quiet and purblind student to gaol for seven years on a charge of wandering around the country at night, ripping open horses, and in the interval writing anonymous letters, many of the most insulting being addressed to himself.'

When Conan Doyle became involved, he corresponded with Edalji about his poor eyesight, and this became one of his main lines of attack. George's eyesight was so bad that it was quite impossible, he claimed, for him to have found his way at night over fields, railway lines, ditches and hedges, between the scene of the outrage of 17 August and the vicarage. 'It must be difficult for him to see objects more than a few inches off,' he wrote, 'and in dusk practically impossible for him to find his way around unfamiliar places.'

Conan Doyle claimed that the report of an occultist, which he had obtained, was alone sufficient to establish Edalji's innocence.

Why had no one thought of this at the trial, with the accused standing in the dock peering through thick lenses?

Being Sherlock Holmes' creator, Conan Doyle felt able to point to someone else as the guilty party, but the name was never revealed, and no one else was ever charged as a result of the famous author's efforts. What did happen, however, was that a commission was appointed to reinvestigate the case. It took its time, but eventually recommended a free pardon for George Edalji. The Home Secretary subsequently felt bound to announce that the Staffordshire police had acted in good faith.

Yet again the Edalji family's delight was short-lived, for it became known that there would be no compensation. Why? Because it was the opinion of the commission that Edalji had actually penned some of the letters himself, this being strongly denied by those who had examined the facts. Even if true, it could not have justified three years penal servitude.

George Edalji said that it was insulting and disgraceful. 'I deny as being false that I wrote the letters or had anything to do with them or the outrages.'

Sir Arthur Conan Doyle declared; 'I differ profoundly on the authorship of the letters of 1903. I say without any reserve that they could not have been written by George Edalji ... there are continual allusions to people and things about which Edalji could have known nothing.

'It is as if there is something mean about the whole business. It is as if they said, "Well, we can't help giving him a free pardon, but you have caused a great deal of trouble and we will take care you get no compensation." '

Clearly overlooked here was the fact that George had never been charged with writing the letters, so to deprive him of compensation on those grounds was a miscarriage of justice. (Incidentally, it transpired that the handwriting expert who had given his condemning opinion against Edalji had been proved wrong at another trial.)

However, George was reinstated to the roll of solicitors, as recommended in the commissioner's report. He no longer lived at Wyrley, but still the maimings went on and the Darby missives continued to appear, the whole combining to keep the name of Edalji and the so-called Wyrley Gang to the fore.

A report of particularly vicious maimings in 1914 at Darlaston provides us with a vivid description of the Black Country generally. 'There is no more desolate stretch of scenery in Great Britain. The very herbage is starved and coarse and blighted. The horizon is ringed with the belching chimneys of a hundred factories and mines: huge pit-banks, miniature mountain ranges of slag and refuse, stand up here and there in bare ugliness.'

This, be it noted, merely a few miles from Great Wyrley in the year of the outbreak of the First World War, no longer quite the rural retreat to which the newly-wed

Edaljis had come to occupy the vicarage in 1874. (The gift of this abode must surely have been the worst wedding present in history!)

It is impossible here to describe the further twists and turns of this story, or even attempt to cover the Darby letters. All that can be said is that in 1915 G. H. Darby, whoever he might have been, wrote promising no more mutilations of cattle during hostilities. Nor were there any!

Was Darby killed at the Front? Did George Edalji ever succeed in receiving compensation? Probably not, with the war taking precedence over all else.

One thing is sure: he and the perhaps mythical Wyrley Gang are still remembered in the lore of the Black Country.

Postscript: Mrs E. Marshall, writer of romantic fiction under the pseudonym Jean Marsh, recalled for me in her ninetieth year (1988) that, when her father was a police superintendent at Halesowen, on the western edge of the Black Country, he was called upon to assist in the hunt for the maimer of horses and cattle, patrolling the fields around Great Wyrley.

11   PC Willitts, Wolverhampton, 1925

A youth spat on the floor of a probation home in Harpenden, near St Albans in Hertfordshire, on Saturday 17 January 1925, and as an indirect result a Wolverhampton policeman lay dying in the gutter at 6.40 the following morning.

PC Albert Willitts, twenty-five years old, with 3½ years service in the Force, reluctantly left his wife and nine-month-old child and set off in the chill darkness along the Willenhall road to report to Bilston Road Police Station, from which he proceeded to traverse his beat, as so often before. It promised to be just another spell of wearisome beat duty, even more unpleasant than usual early on a bleak Sunday morning, when only shift workers at East Wolverhampton's numerous ironworks might be expected to be on the streets, either hurrying to clock on or homeward-bound to their beds, for the roar of the furnaces must never be stilled even though the country was then in a state of depression.

That Willitts was shrewd above the average is evident, for very soon he came upon two young men and a boy, whom he questioned. Dissatisfied with their story, although it transpired that several other officers who had questioned them earlier *had* been satisfied, he decided to follow them. (It is only a short walk from Bilston Road Police Station to Vicarage Road, so it was likely that their aimless wandering around the town had resolved him to act.) When they realized he was on their tail, they began to run. In Vicarage Road he managed to grab one of the youths, and for his diligence he was shot three times, the fatal wound being through the head – from the back.

Several people heard the shots. Jesse Dando, a shop-keeper in Vicarage Road, heard rapid footsteps, 'heavy and light', in the alleyway leading by the side of his house to All Saints Road. Immediately afterwards he heard three shots, and the light footsteps receded. He heard a whistle 'faintly blown', then a groan.

Nurse Skinner, on the staff of the nearby General Hospital, whose sleeping-quarters were in Vicarage Road, was awakened by the shots and also heard the whistle and groan. She looked out of the window and saw two men crossing the road, 'probably youths'.

Thomas Lawley, returning home from work on the night shift, also heard the shots. He found Willitts' body and ran to Bilston Road Police Station to give the alarm. One of the officers who ran to the scene found that Willitts was still alive and trying to say something. Asked about it later in court, he had to admit that he could not understand what Willitts was trying to tell him.

Enquiries were put in hand, and as a result of information from other officers who had seen and spoken to the trio, police set off in cars to patrol the road between Wolverhampton and Stafford. As a result, on that same Sunday afternoon, Inspector Churchward of the Wolverhampton police captured two youths and a boy. They were William Crossley, aged nineteen, a labourer, of Albert Street, Carnforth, Lancashire; Edward Patrick Heggerty, aged seventeen, a waiter of no fixed abode but claiming to be a native of Glasgow, and a fourteen-year-old lad, George James Dixon. They were found to have escaped the previous day from the St Vincent de Paul probation home for boys, Leyton Green, Harpenden, Hertfordshire, a Roman Catholic establishment, opened in 1924 against local opposition by Cardinal Bourne, Archbishop of Westminster. It took twenty-four young boy offenders from London on probation, and closed in 1931.

Crossley and Heggerty were charged jointly with the murder of PC Willitts by shooting him with a revolver. Dixon was sent to a local workhouse, facing a charge in the children's court of attempting to break into a shop at 15 Stafford Road, Wolverhampton. The boy had confessed to the offence, saying, 'I tried to force the door with a piece of iron to get into the shop and get some food. I threw the iron away by the milestone nine miles from Stafford.' He was remanded in custody for seven days.

The two older lads appeared before the magistrates on the Monday, when it was stated by the police that, when formally charged, both had promptly accused the other of the crime.

Heggerty was described as small, with black hair and large eyes under highly arched eyebrows. He bore a nonchalant attitude, had a 'constantly surprised expression' and spoke with a Scottish accent.

Crossley was said to be a well-made youth, a fair young man with a pleasant face, continually moistening his lips. Later, when he shouted out 'offering the court something they did not know', he was declared to have an uncultured voice.

Chief Constable D. Webster, prosecuting, said that he meant only to outline the case and to give sufficient evidence to warrant a remand for one week. He told the court that, from evidence to be produced later, three youths, including the two prisoners, had spoken to Willitts. 'Obviously he had thought their intentions felonious, so he followed them and had them under observation for some forty minutes.'

'It was hard to say whether there had been a struggle,' Webster continued, 'but the constable's clothing was not disarranged, nor were his hands dirty. His helmet had been knocked off and was found lying in the gutter.'

The court was told that, when charged, Heggerty had said, 'It was Crossley who shot him. I saw the flash from the other side of the road. The first shot missed him. I met the kid [Dixon] and heard another shot. Crossley came up and asked if we had heard shots. I said I heard two. I did not tell him I saw him shoot. He said, "It is four." '

Heggerty then told how, as they passed a wood on the Stafford Road, Crossley had thrown something away. 'I thought it was a piece of wood.'

For his part, Crossley insisted, 'I never had the revolver. I don't know how to fire one. I never fired it. Someone else did.'

Dixon had told the police that a revolver had been thrown away along the Stafford Road, and a search was made on that Sunday night with torches, but nothing was found. The next morning Detective Inspector Aston and other officers took Dixon with them in a further attempt to find it, but again without success. Dixon said that tramps – a common enough sight in those days – had been following them and, seeing something thrown away, had investigated and picked it up.

Thus far, all that had been said in court was police evidence, but as Crossley was about to be taken away, he turned and, in the presence of Heggerty, shouted, 'I want to say that Jock [Heggerty] shot him. He fired three shots. I saw the policeman fall. He showed me the revolver near a wood and asked me to throw it away. He threw it away himself. I am telling the truth.'

Crossley blurted out his accusation despite attempts by the clerk of the court to get him to wait until he was legally represented. After the outburst the chief constable stated that Crossley was speaking as an illiterate man ' ... who does not realize what he is charged with'.

The prisoners were then remanded for a week.

The funeral of PC Willitts took place on 22 January, a major event in the town, with flags at half-mast and over 500 police officers following the coffin. Some 4,000 people gathered outside his home as he was taken from there to the great parish church of St Peter. Willitts was a popular officer, of a 'police family'. He had relatives in other local police forces, and they fittingly bore the coffin to its resting-place.

At the resumed hearing on 3 February, young Dixon was the focus of attention as he related how he had seen Willitts catch Crossley by the shoulder and that the latter had jerked his arm and knocked off the officer's helmet. As a result, Willitts had let go of Crossley, catching him again at the crossroads.

By this Dixon meant the junction of Vicarage Road with All Saints Road, not a crossroads unless one counts the alleyway. (I visited the scene whilst writing this (1988) and nothing has changed significantly – the alleyway is still there, as is the nursing home from which Nurse Skinner had peered. But only a few yards nearer the town the area had altered beyond all recognition with the completion in 1987 of the eastern section of the town's ringroad. The streets in the vicinity of the murder have now become a notorious red-light area.)

Continuing his evidence, Dixon explained how, as Willitts was about to regain hold of Crossley, Heggerty came up behind, put his hand in his pocket and pulled out a revolver. 'I saw a flash, the policeman shouted "Help" and as he was going to turn round, Heggerty fired two more shots in quick succession.'

Challenged on this, Heggerty said he had fired at the policeman's legs, '… but my hand was shaky and I fired by his face. I then slipped the revolver into Crossley's pocket and afterwards saw another flash.'

Crossley steadfastly stuck by his story and insisted he had not even known that Heggerty was armed until he fired.

Mr Ross Pashley for the prosecution outlined how the youths had escaped from the home and had arrived in the Midlands by means of 'lorry jumps'. According to Dixon, the revolver was taken from behind a piece of turf on the Luton road where Heggerty had hidden it. It had originally come from a house in London.

Pashley told the court that it did not matter in law, if they were acting in concert, who actually fired the shot! 'Both are equally guilty.' As he went on to outline the case, he referred to an occasion in the police van bringing Heggerty to court from Winson Green Prison where the youths were held, when he had been singing, 'It ain't gonna rain no more'. This irrelevancy caused Heggerty some amusement, as well it might.

At this point neither of the two youths was legally represented, and the magistrate ordered that they be given pencils and paper to enable them to take notes. More information was forthcoming about the escape from the Harpenden home. Heggerty had been admitted there on 5 November 1924, Crossley on 31 December and Dixon on 30 December. On Saturday 17 January 1925, they had gone along the Luton road, and Heggerty had told Dixon to lift a piece of turf concealing a revolver wrapped in rags. He said he wanted it to break into some houses.

The trio had had a lift to Birmingham on a lorry and had walked via West Bromwich to Wolverhampton. At about 4.30 in the morning, Police Constables Green and Lewis saw them. In answer to questions, the trio said that they were going to Stafford, and were believed and allowed to proceed. They had not gone very far when, half an hour later, they were again stopped, this time by Police Sergeant Southwell and a constable. They told the same story and went on their way. Presumably they had told the same story to PC Willitts: he hadn't believed them and had paid with his life.

The officers who had let the lads slip through their fingers no doubt had mixed feelings: egg on the face for not having been more astute, and, at the same time, human nature being what it is, relief that it was not they who had been shot. Of course, the reports given by these officers that the trio had been heading for Stafford led to their undoing and was the reason why they were so quickly arrested. Had they given the slightest thought to their plight, they would have gone anywhere but along the Stafford road, and the way in which they had ambled along after the shooting suggests they had little sense of reality. Could they have been surprised when Inspector Churchward caught up with them and had them back at Wolverhampton Police Station and charged by eleven o'clock that evening?

As so often, such quick work results from the stupidity of the criminal rather than from brilliant police deduction.

Continuing for the prosecution, Pashley said that Dixon would tell the court that, when they realized that Willitts was after them, he had heard Crossley say, 'Shoot him if he gets hold of us, Jock.' Crossley told Dixon to go away, but he only retreated a little way before turning to see what the others were up to.

'Dixon will tell you,' droned Pashley, 'that he saw Willitts quicken his steps, cross over the road and get hold of Crossley, and saw the latter knock his helmet off. It fell into the left-hand gutter. Dixon's story was corroborated to the extent that the helmet was indeed found there.'

Thus was the seed planted that Dixon was to be believed.

According to Dixon, the two youths had caught him up immediately after the shooting, and Crossley had said to him, 'If you tell the police anything that will lead us to being in prison, we will shoot you.'

On the road to Stafford they had attempted to dispose of the revolver. First, Crossley had thrown it through the window of some houses under construction, then thought better of it and retrieved it. Finally, he had, according to Dixon, flung it into a wood.

The prosecution was full of what Dixon would say even to the fact that he had seen three tramps following and one of them might have picked up the revolver, which was not found. He went on to say that on their way back to Wolverhampton after their capture, Heggerty had said to Crossley, 'RFA me', to which Crossley had replied,

'RFA me, Jock.' It was explained that this was a slang term and meant Ready For Anything'.

Interviewed by Detective Inspector Aston, Heggerty stated that Crossley was blaming it all on him. 'I only did part of it. I don't know where the revolver came from. A boy named Don O'Leary put it in my pocket just before we all ran away. It was a six-chamber revolver, fully loaded, and was of blue steel with a wooden handle.'

Heggerty said that they were making for Lancaster, '... where Crossley was going to show me a house we could break in to, as the woman had no legs, but her husband was a millionaire'.

Despite what Heggerty now said about the revolver, it transpired that he had earlier told the police how he had got it from a man named O'Leary, who lived at Amshurst Park, Stamford Hill, London, where it was kept in a black box. Pashley said that he only mentioned this because the police had checked and found that a man named O'Leary lived at that address and had seen a black box as described.

The prosecution concluded by asking the jury to commit both youths to the next Staffordshire Assizes, for the wilful murder of PC Willitts.

The Wolverhampton police surgeon then took the stand and described his post-mortem examination of Willitts. 'There was a wound two inches long across the left temple, but the bone was not penetrated. At the back of the head there was a punctured wound and further investigation revealed two pieces of metal embedded in the skull, and a bullet in the brain.'

The three pieces of metal were exhibited.

Next in the witness-box was Frederick Sear, superintendent of the St Vincent de Paul hostel in Harpenden. He knew the prisoners and the boy Dixon. In reply to a question by Crossley, he agreed that he had never seen him with a revolver.

George James Dixon then caused a ripple in the court

with his appearance. He held the key to the situation, his testimony well heralded! He said he was an orphan and had met Crossley and Heggerty for the first time when he was sent to the home. He corroborated Pashley's statement about obtaining the revolver from beneath turf, and described their journey to Wolverhampton.

Cross-examined by Crossley, Dixon said he had seen him with a revolver.

Crossley: 'When did you see me with it?'

Dixon: 'In the house where we slept' (after the crime).

Crossley: 'That's all lies.'

Joseph Homer, a motor engineer of Hockley, Birmingham, then came to the stand and told how he had given the boy Dixon a lift between Dunstable and Coventry. He did not know that the two prisoners were also on the lorry but remembered having seen them at a coffee stall at Weedon, where he stopped.

Various witnesses then trooped in for their brief statements: Thomas Lawley, who had heard three shots, found the dying constable and gone for help; the officer on duty at the police station when Lawley arrived, and the officers who had spoken to the youths at points in their journey prior to the murder. The naïvety of one of them was obvious when he said he had seen Heggerty apparently lame and supported by the others. In explanation, Heggerty had told them he had gout.

Gout! Hardly likely in a seventeen-year-old!

Detective Inspector Aston then related how Crossley and Heggerty had blamed each other. As the pair were having their fingerprints taken, Crossley had blurted out, 'I ain't going to swing for him!' (Heggerty) Aston had urged him to be quiet and reserve his defence, but Crossley had replied, 'I don't care. He's a liar. You can catch a thief, but you can't catch a liar. I am a good Catholic and I want to ease my soul.'

Aston then told him to write it down, but Crossley said he could not write and asked the inspector to write it for him. This was done, and it was produced in court and read out by the clerk.

'Of my own free will,' Crossley's statement began, 'I want to tell what happened when the policeman was shot. I first met Jock Heggerty in the home about a fortnight ago and got to know him. At about half-past ten on Saturday morning 17 January me, him and Dixon decided to run away to Lancaster to look for some work. I left the home because someone had spit on the floor and I got blamed for it.'

Having detailed the journey to Wolverhampton and the shooting, Crossley said he had asked Heggerty why he had done it and told him he was a fool. 'I've a good mind to give you away when we see another policeman,' and Heggerty had replied, 'You can do what you like.'

His statement concluded with the business of disposing of the gun along the Stafford road shortly before they were arrested.

After revealing to the court that every pond, ditch and hedge on the Stafford road had been searched without finding a trace of the revolver, the case for the prosecution was concluded.

However, Crossley was not done and elected to give further evidence, declaring he was not going to take the blame, and in a long rambling off-the-cuff statement avoided all that was alleged to have happened. 'It was all lies what they had said before. None of them had shot PC Willitts.'

The bench apparently suffered his nonsensical diatribe without interruption. They then committed the two men for trial at the next assizes.

News was scarce at the beginning of 1925, so that the case continued to receive prominence. However, one interesting little item serves to highlight, and indeed to prove, the existence of the Black Country custom of wife-selling. On 20 January it was reported that a woman who had just died at Bilston had been sold some years earlier to a lodger for sixpence. Not only had the ertswhile husband and purchaser gone to the nearest public house to 'wet the deal', but a receipt had been made out and signed. Now that the woman had died and left some money, the question arose as to who should have it. The husband said he had disposed only of his wife, not of her possessions.

One does not know the outcome, but this is certainly one of the last examples of a practice thought to have died out much earlier. At one time widespread, wife-selling was a simple, mutually agreed method of separation, since divorce was out of the question for working people.

The trial of Crossley and Heggerty opened at Stafford on 27 February before Mr Justice Salter (1850-1928), said to have a brain of the 'highest calibre … his judgements containing no unnecessary words', with Sir Reginald Coventry and Mr W. Hudson for the Crown. Messrs Sharp & Millichip of West Bromwich (still in business there) instructed Mr Clements to defend Crossley, and Mr Wood, Heggerty.

Outlining the case, Sir Reginald stressed persistently how the two youths blamed each other for the crime, repeating their contradictory statements.

'The jury,' he declared, 'may have difficulty in determining who actually fired the revolver, but will have no difficulty in coming to the conclusion that one or other of them was responsible for the murder of PC Willitts. It would not be necessary for them to decide who actually pulled the trigger. Both prisoners were equally guilty of murder.'

Most people listening would have known that; what made them sit up was when he went on to say: 'If the prosecution was correct that the boys [as he called them] walked out from the home on an adventure armed with a revolver loaded in case of emergency, then the young lad Dixon is as guilty as the other two. If that is the case, then the evidence he would give should be looked at with suspicion. Nobody,' he added, 'suggested that Dixon had fired at the policeman.'

The prosecution then put Dixon forward as a witness, whereupon the defending counsel for Crossley caused a stir in the court by asking: 'Am I right that the case against Dixon has been dropped in order that he can give evidence?' The short answer 'yes' must have dashed any lingering hope the prisoners may have had, for here was their travelling-companion, the one person in a position to say precisely what had happened, now prepared to turn King's Evidence.

Dixon related what had been disclosed by statement at the magistrates' court. Cross-examined by Mr Clements as to when he first heard of a revolver, Dixon said, 'Whilst at the home. Jock wanted a stick of dynamite, a flash-lamp and a revolver to break into some houses.'

Asked about the incident when the revolver was picked up, he said that he and Heggerty had held a whispered conversation. Clements seized on this. 'Didn't you whisper because you didn't want Crossley to hear?'

'No, sir. Jock told Crossley he had a revolver. Jock was his best pal.'

Cross-examined by Mr Wood, for Heggerty, as to why he had tried to recover the revolver after Crossley had thrown it away the first time along the Stafford road, Dixon said it was because he wanted to hand it to the police.

On this unlikely statement the case for the Crown came to an end.

The defence line of approach became apparent immediately, when Clements revealed that, whilst in custody, the prisoners were examined by a doctor. When the judge said that he had the doctor's report, Clements asked for the doctor to be put in the witness-box. The intention to cast doubt upon the sanity of the two men was obvious, but the prosecution would have none of it. It was not thought necessary, Sir Reginald declared.

Clements then called Crossley, who again gave his version of the shooting, stoutly denying prior knowledge of the revolver. He admitted lying at the magistrate's court when he said that no one had shot the policeman. He had done this because he had heard one of the policemen present say it was best to hang them both.

In his evidence, Heggerty admitted having fired the first shot, which missed. He said he then walked to Crossley, who took the revolver and fired a shot. 'Probably due to two shots being fired in quick succession, it sounded like one.'

Heggerty also said that they had stopped Dixon from getting hold of the revolver after it was thrown away the first time because, '... if he had got it, and had done anything with it, then we should have been blamed'.

Sir Reginald Coventry put it to him that he had always wanted to possess a revolver.

'Only lately.'

'Why?'

'To rob somebody.'

'You shot at a policeman?'

'Yes, sir.'

'And you killed him?'

'No, sir.'

'What did you mean to do?'

'Only frighten him.'

Following this exchange, no further evidence was called for the defence.

In his summing-up the judge communicated to the jury the gist of the medical report mentioned earlier. Crossley was said to have the intelligence of a child of nine years. However, the result was in little doubt, and the jury took only thirty minutes to reach a verdict of guilty.

Both men were sentenced to death.

An appeal was lodged, supported by a petition signed by a large number of people, living at Lancaster and Carnforth, the latter being Crossley's home town. His supporters apparently cared more about the outcome than did Heggerty's family and friends in Glasgow, whose efforts on his behalf, if any, went unreported.

Meanwhile, at Wolverhampton, a fund set up by the local newspaper to assist PC Willitts' widow was kept to the fore, and a celebrity concert was planned for 26 March.

By the day of the appeal – 23 March – Wolverhampton had just suffered its coldest weekend of the year, and the papers were full of German peace pact proposals which would lead to the signing of the Locarno Pact later in the year, following which Germany was admitted to the League of Nations. (In 1936 the Nazis were formally to denounce the pact; with the ongoing consequences of that denunciation we are all only too familiar.)

The appeal failed despite a valiant attempt by Kenneth Wood for Heggerty. He said that Heggerty had fired the first shot, which missed, and Crossley had fired the others. The proper verdict in the circumstances should have been manslaughter. 'It was not cold-blooded murder. The shooting was on the spur of the moment.'

The execution was fixed for 7 April, and as March came to an end, the two young men must have given up hope of a reprieve. However, on April Fool's day, the Home Secretary, Sir William Joyson-Hicks (successively Post Master General, Minister of Health and Home Secretary between 1924 and 1929) commuted their sentence to that of life imprisonment.

The shooting of a police officer was extremely rare in those days, and public indignation ran high. They were lucky to escape the noose and, assuming they were imprisoned for, say, twelve years, did they perhaps use their freedom to redeem themselves during World War II?

Afterword

There are of course more recent murders of note either in or on the fringe of the Black Country than those dealt with here. One recalls, for example, the battering to death of Dorothy Mills, a West Bromwich spinster in her thirties, but the murderer was never found and the prime suspect may still be alive. Again, there is the murder in 1978 of the Wordsley (Stourbridge) newsboy Carl Bridgewater, but the crime is well documented and the convicted men are still (1988) protesting their innocence.

Even the notorious Donald Neilson (Black Panther) committed one of his crimes in the region, shooting a security guard at the then Dudley Freightliner Terminal. The victim lived for some time afterwards, and Neilson was not charged with his murder, although readers will no doubt recall his other awful deeds, principally the kidnapping and murder of Lesley Whittle, a one-time student at Wolverhampton Polytechnic.

On the mystery side, one has the intriguing case of a female skeleton found in a wych-elm at Hagley, near Stourbridge, by boys on a bird-nesting expedition. The discovery created great excitement and speculation, but the year was 1943 and the momentous events of war soon pushed the story into the background. But how, why and where Bella – as the victim came to be called – met her fate, remains a mystery to this day.

In recent decades, one has read the reports of Black Country murders – invariably due to spontaneous acts of violence – almost daily. By comparison, the period covered in this book was not, for all its hardships, overtly murder-riven.

Readers may well feel surprise at the kindliness frequently displayed by the police in days gone by towards men who were clearly guilty of a capital crime but had yet to face trial. Some prisoners were even allowed to leave their cells to sit by the fire in an inspector's office.

The courteous, meticulous way in which hearings and trials were conducted is also noteworthy and fair-mindedness was paramount, save apparently in the case of George Edalji (Chapter 10).

What came over strongly to me in the researching and writing is the fact that hanging proved to be no deterrent since, with the exception of the unknown killer(s) of Kent Reeks (Chapter 8), none of the murderers tried to evade capture, and indeed one of them promptly sought a policeman and gave himself up. Even as recently as 1957 Dennis Howard (Chapter 5) could have shot his way to at least temporary freedom, yet forbore to do so.

Now that hanging is abolished one may only surmise whether those who commit murder today would allow themselves to be captured so readily, if they knew they were likely to be hanged. Probably not, since there are instances of murderers promptly killing themselves rather than face even long-term prison sentences.

Certainly the murderers in this volume did not see 'the rope' dangling before their eyes when they set upon their victims.

Index